WISDOM TEXTS FROM QUMRAN

This study is the first full analysis of the Qumran wisdom texts. New translations and a full explanation of the background and context of wisdom literature introduce the reader to an important and hitherto little discussed part of the Dead Sea Scrolls.

After surveying biblical and extrabiblical wisdom books, the author considers the best and most fully preserved wisdom texts from Qumran. The centrepiece of the book is a discussion of the large wisdom instruction known as Sapiential Work A. In addition, the author reflects on the relevance of those texts for the study of early Judaism and Christianity. An appendix treats the Ben Sira scroll from Masada.

Daniel J. Harrington, S. J., is Professor of New Testament at Weston Jesuit School of Theology in Cambridge, Massachusetts. He is the author of *The Maccabean Revolt* (1988), *The Gospel of Matthew* (1991) and *Paul on the Mystery of Israel* (1992).

This new series, *The Literature of the Dead Sea Scrolls*, provides in six volumes an overall introduction to the principal kinds of literature amongst the Dead Sea Scrolls. Since all the unpublished texts came into the public domain in 1991, there has been much scholarly activity in editing the materials. However, little has been published to provide the interested student with a concise guide to the complete extant literary corpus. This new series aims to fill that gap through its popular presentation of the main ideas and concerns of the literature from Qumran and elsewhere in the Judaean wilderness.

The series is intended for all interested in the Dead Sea Scrolls, especially undergraduate and graduate students working in Biblical Studies or the study of Jewish history and religion in the late Second Temple period. Written by the foremost experts in their particular fields, the series serves to advance general knowledge of the scrolls and to inform the discussion of the background to the self-definition of early Judaism and nascent Christianity.

WISDOM TEXTS
FROM QUMRAN

Daniel J. Harrington, S. J.

London and New York

First published 1996
by Routledge
11 New Fetter Lane, London EC4P 4EE

Simultaneously published in the USA and Canada
by Routledge
29 West 35th Street, New York, NY 10001

Typeset in Garamond by
Datix International Limited, Bungay, Suffolk

Printed and bound in Great Britain by Redwood Books, Trowbridge,
Wiltshire

British Library Cataloguing in Publication Data
A catalogue for this book is available from the British Library

Library of Congress Cataloguing-in-Publication Data
Harrington, Daniel J.
Wisdom texts from Qumran / Daniel J. Harrington.
p.   cm. – (Literature of the Dead Sea scrolls)
Includes bibliographical references and index.
1. Dead Sea scrolls–Criticism, interpretation, etc.   2. Wisdom
literature–Criticism, interpretation, etc.   3. Wisdom–Religious
aspects–Judaism.   I. Title.   II. Series.
BM487.H29   1996   96-354
296. 1'55–dc20

ISBN 0-415-13906-6 (hbk)
ISBN 0-415-13907-4 (pbk)

TO JOHN STRUGNELL

CONTENTS

SERIES EDITOR'S PREFACE

The Literature of the Dead Sea Scrolls is a six-volume series designed to provide introductions to the principal literary genres found among these very important texts. From the outset the intention behind the series has been to focus on the texts themselves, before trying to assert what their historical or theological significance might be. The series treats principally the finds from the eleven caves at Qumran, but some other contemporary texts found in the Judaean wilderness in the last fifty years are also considered

In 1991 all the unpublished manuscripts from caves 4 and 11 at Qumran became available to the scholarly world at large and to the general public. Much has been done to incorporate all the new information into scholarly debates about Jewish religion and history in the late Second Temple period, but little of the overall significance of the whole literary corpus has been put in the public domain. A major aim of this series is to step back from the debates about the history and identification of the community or movement responsible for writing or preserving these manuscripts. In so doing, entirely fresh consideration can be given to the literary corpus as a whole within the context of Jewish literature of the three centuries before the fall of the temple in 70 CE. On such fresh and newly constructed foundations firmer opinions can be offered about the importance of the scrolls for emerging forms of Judaism and for nascent Christianity.

It is important for those interested in Jewish history and religion of this period to have access to the primary resources, the texts, for themselves, so that anybody can make up their own minds about them. However, some of the textual evidence is very fragmentary and difficult to assess, some of it is entirely new evidence in the discussions. Students of all kinds need straightforward guides to the literature to enable them to trace a secure path through the mass of material. It is not the purpose of this series to provide detailed translations and commentaries on individual texts, though in some chapters of some of the volumes in the series this is the case. Though small extracts and quotations are often given, to make the most of what is written in each volume readers will need to have access to one of the standard translations of the Dead Sea scrolls in English. Nor is the purpose of the series to cover every single text. But the general reader will find here a valuable and up-to-date companion to the principal literary genres found in the scrolls.

Such companions as these may be especially useful to those studying similiar genres in related fields such as the Hebrew Bible, the New Testament, or Jewish halakhah, so that those too are not studied in isolation from this extensive literary corpus which provides so much insight into the development of genres in the period.

I am grateful to my colleagues in the field of Dead Sea scrolls research who have taken the time to contribute to this worthwhile venture and to the editors at Routledge, especially Richard Stoneman, for the enthusiastic welcome given to this series and its individual volumes.

George Brooke

ACKNOWLEDGEMENTS

When I accepted the invitation to work with my former doctoral mentor and longtime friend, John Strugnell, on editing wisdom texts from Qumran (4Q415-418) for the Discoveries in the Judaean Desert Series, I also had the dream of writing a synthetic book on wisdom at Qumran for a general audience. The invitation to be part of this series from Professor George J. Brooke has happily turned a vague wish into a concrete reality. I thank Professor Brooke for his very practical advice and careful reading of my manuscript. He has been extraordinarily helpful to me. I also thank Richard Stoneman of Routledge for his patience and direction. Help on word-processing matters came at various points from my friends at the Weston Jesuit School of Theology, Terry Lima, Chris Matthews, and Tom Williams.

My greatest debt of gratitude, however, is owed to John Strugnell. Each Sunday afternoon for the past several years we have met to discuss the progress of our editorial work and to go for a walk. From our common work and our conversations I have learned much about the Dead Sea scrolls from a scholar whose knowledge and love of these texts have few rivals. And so I dedicate this book in gratitude to John Strugnell.

1

INTRODUCTION TO WISDOM AT QUMRAN

INTRODUCTION

It has long been recognized that the foundational documents of the Qumran library – works such as the Community Rule, Damascus Document, and Thanksgiving Hymns – contain wisdom elements. Likewise, it has long been known that small fragments of the biblical wisdom books – Proverbs, Job, Qohelet, and Sirach – were discovered at Qumran. But the Qumran library has yielded still other Jewish wisdom texts from the Second Temple period (537 BCE to 70 CE). A few of these were previously known in ancient translations, but most of them were previously unknown. The focus of this study is the corpus of newly discovered (since 1947) wisdom texts from Qumran, though it will also relate these texts to the biblical wisdom books and to what are regarded as "sectarian" works in the Qumran library. Finally, it will consider what contributions these Qumran wisdom texts might make to illumining the development of early Judaism and the place of the Qumran community within it, and the development of early Christianity and the figure of Jesus.

Wisdom at Qumran is a relatively new topic on the agenda of Dead Sea scrolls research (Lipscomb and Sanders 1977: 277–85). It has come to prominence most obviously because in recent years the photographs of all the Qumran manuscripts have become generally available, and among these manuscripts there are wisdom texts. It is also part of a more general resurgence of interest in the biblical and extrabiblical wisdom books, inspired in part by claims that Jesus should be viewed as a Jewish wisdom teacher, and in part by feminist interest in the figure of Sophia.

What do the Qumran wisdom texts say? What contributions do

these texts make to our understanding of biblical wisdom, early Judaism, and Jesus and Christian origins? This guide to the Qumran wisdom writings seeks to answer such questions. It is intended for theological students and biblical scholars, not so much for specialists in the Dead Sea scrolls. It focuses on the best and most fully preserved wisdom texts from Qumran. Using the tools of literary analysis and with a particular concern for theological significance, it offers new translations along with a serious and sympathetic reading of the Qumran wisdom texts. Its goal is to uncover and make clear what these texts say. The presentation on the whole moves from the more familiar to more recently available Qumran texts, and from the more generically Second Temple Jewish texts to the more "sectarian" texts.

PRESUPPOSITIONS AND PROCEDURES

At the outset, I feel the need to state my historical presuppositions about these texts and the place at which they were found from 1947 onward. I regard the Qumran scrolls as the remnants of the library of a Jewish religious movement that had a center at Qumran between the second century BCE and the first century CE. I believe that there is a relation between the ancient library of Qumran and the remains of the buildings at Qumran. I consider these buildings to have been more like a religious retreat house or a monastery than an army camp – though I admit that none of these analogies may do full justice to what went on at Qumran. And finally, I accept the identification of this Jewish religious movement as Essene, or at least as a group akin to what ancient writers said about the Essenes in the Dead Sea area.

The specificity of my presuppositions about the Dead Sea scrolls, which many scholars share (Cross 1995; Fitzmyer 1992b; VanderKam 1994) raises a problem for the exposition of the Qumran wisdom texts. If the Dead Sea scrolls represent the remnants of an Essene library, how can one distinguish what texts are specific to and distinctive of the Essene movement from what they may have regarded merely as pious and appropriate reading ("library books")?

My personal situation can illustrate the problem. As a member of the Society of Jesus (a Catholic religious order), I have in my room official Jesuit documents and works of Jesuit spirituality, Catholic church documents and books of Catholic theology, and all sorts of biblical tools and monographs, as well as a few novels and a history of American baseball. What interpretation might an archaeologist 2,000 years from now give to this collection? An analogous problem faces students of the Dead Sea scrolls in general and of the Qumran wisdom texts in particular. How do we know what the Qumran people regarded as important among their books?

I will try to deal with this problem by first acknowledging it and by being cautious. The collection of wisdom texts from Qumran at the very least shows what members of the movement thought worth obtaining, reading, and preserving, and perhaps also worth integrating into their own theology and practice.

The wisdom books contained in the Jewish and Christian canons of Scripture were part of the Qumran library – though they are not nearly as well represented as the Law and the Prophets are. There are fragments of Proverbs (4Q102–103), Job (4Q99–101), Qohelet (4Q109–110), and Sirach/Ecclesiasticus/Ben Sira (2Q18 and 11Q5 Sirach [= Sirach 51:13–19b, 30]), as well as 4Q and 11Q Targums of Job. What follows is a guide to the biblical and nonbiblical wisdom texts among the Qumran scrolls.

The order of the texts and expositions is not chronological. Indeed, determining the precise chronology of the Qumran wisdom texts is difficult, if not impossible. There are no clear references in them to contemporary historical events or persons. The archaeological evidence, Carbon 14 testing, and palaeography (the study of ancient scripts) all indicate that the Qumran manuscripts in general were written between the second century BCE and the first century CE. On the basis of palaeographical analysis the manuscripts of the Qumran wisdom texts have mainly been assigned to the first century BCE and the first half of the first century CE. Of course, palaeographic analysis establishes only the dates of particular manuscripts, not those of the autographs. It can tell us the date after which a work could not have been composed. But when exactly the work was first written is more difficult to say. Nevertheless I am quite confident that the Qumran wisdom texts treated in this volume originated in the second and first centuries BCE.

The order is basically pedagogical. Since the Qumran wisdom texts did not arise in an intellectual vacuum, we begin with a survey of pertinent biblical wisdom texts. They can help us to see what is common sapiential material and what may be distinctive in the

Qumran documents. Then we consider biblical wisdom texts and targums found at Qumran. Next we look at some wisdom texts from the great Cave 11 Psalms Scroll. These have been available for thirty years and do not seem to be distinctively "Qumranian." Then we examine two texts from Cave 4: a poem on Lady Folly (4Q184) and part of a wisdom instruction (4Q185). The centerpiece of this book is the wisdom instruction contained in the Sapiential Work A (1Q26, 4Q415–418, 423). Then we deal with various other Qumran wisdom texts, and investigate the sapiential elements in well known "sectarian" texts, such as Community Rule and Thanksgiving Hymns (found not only in Cave 1 but also in Cave 4). We conclude with reflections on the contributions that these Qumran texts make to the study of early Judaism and the Qumran community, as well as early Christianity. Since Ben Sira's wisdom book is roughly contemporary with the Qumran texts, we have included an appendix on the nature and importance of the Hebrew version found at Masada.

The translations of biblical texts are taken from the New Revised Standard Version. This is a widely available and generally reliable translation, though its policy of gender-inclusive language sometimes distorts the "masculine" language of the wisdom writings.

The references to the Qumran texts follow the usual conventions. Thus, 4Q416 2 iii 4 refers to Text 416 from Qumran Cave 4, fragment 2, column iii, line 4. In some cases (especially in texts from Cave 1), I have used the common designations: 1QS (Rule of the Community), 1QSa (Appendix A to 1QS), and 1QH (Hodayot, or Thanksgiving Hymns). The italic numbers in the translations refer to line numbers, and the square brackets with three dots indicate a gap in the manuscript.

Since many of the Qumran wisdom texts are difficult to translate and are not readily available to nonspecialists, I have included translations of the most important texts and fragments along with my expositions of them. The translations are basically my own. Of course, I have been helped greatly by the translations by Geza Vermes (1995), Florentino García Martínez (1994), James A. Sanders (1965, 1967), and especially John Strugnell.

As I said, the wisdom texts from Qumran did not arise in an intellectual and religious vacuum. Rather, they arose in a society and culture in which the ideas and literary forms of wisdom writings were well known. And so in order to appreciate what is new and important about the wisdom texts from Qumran, we must first place them in the context of wisdom texts in ancient Israel, with particular attention to what elements are most significant for understanding the Qumran texts.

2

ISRAEL'S WISDOM TRADITION

INTRODUCTION

In that part of the Hebrew Bible known traditionally as the "Writings" there are three wisdom books – Proverbs, Qohelet (its Hebrew name) or Ecclesiastes (its Greek name), and Job, as well as some "wisdom psalms." The wider canon represented by the Greek Septuagint version contains two more wisdom books – Sirach or Ecclesiasticus (the Greek version of the Hebrew wisdom book by Ben Sira of Jerusalem that was translated by his grandson in Egypt), and the Wisdom of Solomon (which was composed in Greek). To appreciate the tradition in which the Qumran wisdom texts stand and to understand their distinctive or particular character, it is important at the outset to give a brief survey of Israel's wisdom tradition as it is expressed in these writings and as it relates to the Qumran wisdom texts.

Israel's wisdom was part of an international movement that also found literary expressions in ancient Egypt and Mesopotamia. Such wisdom was mainly concerned with human relations and humankind's place within creation. Its goal was to show people how to cope with life – how to avoid obstacles and dangers, and thus how to find human wholeness and happiness. Human experience provided the raw material for the ancient wisdom teachers, and their task was to evaluate that experience in the light of practical reason and to express it in short sayings that would help others to deal with life as they found it. These sages did not generally claim their authority from divine revelation.

The wisdom teachers of Israel shared, or more likely took over, the results of the activity of the ancient Near Eastern sages. But the Israelite sages integrated these materials into their own distinctive theological framework. Israel's clear idea of its God as both the creator of heaven and earth, and the God who had entered into covenant relationship with Israel, gave a peculiar focus to Israelite wisdom. Some biblical traditions made King Solomon into the model and patron of wisdom (see 1 Kings 4:29–34), and viewed the whole world and the human experience of it and within it as the God of Israel's creation. The starting point, content, and goal of Israel's wisdom was "fear of the Lord" – the proper respect for and awe before God based upon an accurate perception of who God is and who human beings are in the presence of God.

The Jewish wisdom books are generally acknowledged today to have been put in their present form in post-exilic times (after 587 BCE). Qohelet is confidently assigned to the third century BCE, and Sirach can be dated around 180 BCE. Wisdom is usually located in Alexandria in the first century BCE. Job may reflect an attempt to deal with Israel's experience of defeat, destruction, and exile in the sixth century BCE and afterward. Proverbs is a large collection of several smaller collections. Though it may contain some pre-exilic material, it was most likely put into its present form after the exile. All this means that the Qumran wisdom writings were part of larger post-exilic Jewish movements toward collecting and codifying Israel's wisdom during the so-called Second Temple period.

Where precisely this Israelite wisdom originated and developed is difficult to say. Some biblical wisdom teachings presuppose a setting in the family or in the clan, whereas other teachings fit better in the royal court or in schools. Indeed, all three life-settings – family, royal court, and school – probably contributed to Israel's wisdom writings.

Wisdom teachings in Israel generally took the form of poetry – short parallel sayings in which the basic point is made twice – either in similar ways (synonymous parallelism) or in opposing ways (antithetical parallelism). These teachings might be expressed in several ways. Some are in free-standing sayings on various topics (as in much of Proverbs 10–31). Some are in collections of sayings on the same basic topics (as in Sirach, Qohelet, and parts of Proverbs). There are instructions introduced by "my son" or similar addresses (as in Proverbs 1–9 and 22:17–24:22, and Sirach). And there are even acrostic poems with each unit introduced by a new letter of the Hebrew alphabet (Prov 31:10–31; see also Psalm 119).

A full discussion of ancient Israel's wisdom literature would be out of place in this short introduction to the Qumran wisdom writings. And there already are many excellent introductions to the biblical wisdom books (Clements 1992; Crenshaw 1981; Gammie and Perdue 1990; Murphy 1981, 1990; Perdue *et al.* 1993; Westermann 1994). What follows is merely an attempt to set the stage for wisdom texts found at Qumran. Here I want to point out what in the biblical wisdom books is most important for understanding the Qumran wisdom texts. Proverbs, Sirach, and 1 Enoch are basic resources. The wisdom psalms, Qohelet, Job, and the Wisdom of Solomon are less relevant to our task.

MAJOR RESOURCES

Proverbs

The most obvious contribution of the book of Proverbs to understanding Qumran wisdom is the sapiential vocabulary. The prologue to Proverbs (1:2–7) contains the words that are all over the Qumran wisdom texts: wisdom, instruction, understanding, wise dealing, righteousness, justice, equity, shrewdness, knowledge, prudence, learning, skill, and so forth. There are two kinds of people: the wise and the foolish. The prologue links the search for wisdom with Israel's God ("fear of the Lord"), history (the ascription to Solomon), and ethical values ("righteousness, justice, and equity"). These links are generally taken for granted in the Qumran wisdom texts.

The book of Proverbs also introduces matters of form and content that are prominent in Qumran wisdom writings. The wisdom poems in chapters 1–9 take the form of instructions from an elder sage or father to a young man or son who needs instruction: "Hear, my son. . . ." Most of them portray Wisdom as a personal (female) figure issuing an invitation to learn wisdom. Fools and simpletons reject the call of Lady Wisdom, whereas the wise heed it and act upon it. The evil counterpart of Lady Wisdom is the "foreign" or "loose" woman – Lady Folly, who leads fools astray and ultimately to their death (see 9:18).

Lady Wisdom had a pivotal role in creation: "The Lord by wisdom founded the earth" (3:19). The famous poem in Proverbs 8:22–31, which has exercised such an enormous influence on later Jewish and early Christian writings, first (8:22–26) portrays wisdom as having been created before anything else: "The Lord created me at (or, as) the beginning of his work, the first of his acts of long ago." It then (8:27–31) describes Wisdom's role in the process of creation: "I was beside him, like a master worker (or, little child), and I was daily his delight, rejoicing before him always."

A glance at the main collection of 375 sayings in Proverbs 10:1–22:16 reveals topics that are prominent in Sapiential Work A and other Qumran texts: honesty in business dealings, paying back loans quickly, the bad effects of greed, the need for avoiding foolish and evil persons, care and caution in social relations, right practices in family relationships (husbands and wives, parents and children), and the rewards of wise/righteous actions and the punishments for foolish/evil actions.

The instructions in Proverbs 22:17–24:22 ("the words of the wise"), which themselves may have been based on the Egyptian Instruction of Amenemopet, seem to have provided the formal model for the Sapiential Work A and other wisdom instructions. The experienced sage gives advice in the second person singular in the form of prohibitions ("Do not rob the poor") or imperatives ("Apply your mind to instruction") on a variety of practical topics: oppressing the poor, friendship, standing surety, moving boundaries, table manners, and so on. The acrostic poem about the good wife (or Wisdom?) in Proverbs 31:10–31 describes what a positive asset "a woman who fears the Lord" can be to her husband.

Sirach

Much of what has been said about the value of Proverbs for understanding Qumran wisdom can be said also about Sirach. It too is full of wisdom terminology, and the contrast between the wise and the foolish. It links wisdom traditions even more explicitly with the legal, historical, and prophetic strands of the biblical tradition. Its most common setting is the instruction addressed to "my son." It too gives teachings on money matters, friendship, social relations, family relations (husbands and wives, parents and children), happiness, and rewards and punishments. Many of these topics are also treated in the Qumran Sapiential Work A and other wisdom instructions (Lehmann 1961: 103–16).

There are at least three areas in which Sirach especially illumines the Qumran wisdom texts. Following Proverbs 8:22–31, Ben Sira writes a beautiful poem in praise of Wisdom as a female figure present at creation and dwelling in Israel at the Jerusalem Temple (Sirach

24:1–22). He then makes an equation between Wisdom and the Torah: "All this is the book of the covenant of the Most High God, the Law that Moses commanded us as an inheritance for the congregations of Israel" (24:23). Moreover, Ben Sira's "autobiographical" poem about his search for Wisdom portrayed as a female (51:13–30) appears separately in the Psalms Scroll from Qumran Cave 11 (discussed separately in Chapter 4).

A second area is the lively interest in the cosmos. In one sense, all wisdom teaching reflects on the order of creation. But in three long poems (16:24–18:14; 39:12–35; 42:15–43:33) Ben Sira gives particular attention to God's wisdom as displayed in the cosmos. Some of the Qumran writings show an analogous interest in the cosmos as a theological framework for wisdom instruction. There is, however, far more concern with eschatology at Qumran than in Sirach (see, however, Sirach 36:1–22).

A third area is theodicy. To defend the sovereignty of God and to allow for the existence of evil within God's creation, Ben Sira developed the doctrine of the pairs: "See now all the works of the Most High: they come in pairs, the one the opposite of the other" (33:15) . . . ; "All of them come in twos, one corresponding to the other; yet none of them has He made in vain" (42:14). This duality within creation that Ben Sira postulates somewhat timidly is further developed in the Qumran writings to reach a modified dualism according to which God presides over a creation given over to two powers (the Angel of Light and the Prince of Darkness) until the final visitation that will vindicate the righteous and destroy the wicked. For the fullest explanation of this theological interpretation of creation, history, and eschatology, see the "Instruction on the Two Spirits" in the Community Rule iii 13–iv 25. This framework of modified dualism seems to be the assumption underlying at least some of the Qumran wisdom writings and the "sectarian writings."

1 Enoch

Although not part of the traditional biblical canon (except in the Ethiopic Orthodox church), the collection known as 1 Enoch (Knibb 1984: 169–319) also qualifies as a major resource for understanding wisdom at Qumran. The collection consists of five "booklets": the Book of Watchers (chs 1–36), the Book of Parables or Similitudes (37–71), the Astronomical Book (72–82), the Book of

Dreams (83–90), and the Epistle of Enoch (91–107). Fragments of about twenty manuscripts of all these booklets except the Similitudes were found at Qumran (Milik 1976). The so-called Book of Giants may have occupied the place of the Similitudes in the five-booklet collection.

The abundance of manuscript evidence for 1 Enoch at Qumran suggests that it was an important and popular book there. Some manuscripts antedate the settlement at Qumran (mid-second century BCE). The work may have served merely as "pious reading" for the Qumran community. Yet the many linguistic parallels and the insistence on the 364-day solar calendar indicate that 1 Enoch arose in circles more directly related to the Qumran group, perhaps even in the "parent" movement from which the Qumran community evolved. However, the fact that some of the 1 Enoch manuscripts were re-used for other works suggests that there may have been less interest in it at a later time.

For the study of Qumran wisdom 1 Enoch (leaving chs 37–71 out of consideration) is important first of all because of its insistence on God's wisdom about human history as something heavenly and esoteric. Therefore, the mysterious biblical figure of Enoch (see Gen 5:21–24) is granted "a holy vision in the heavens . . . for a distant generation which will come" (1:2). He is also given access to "the tablets of heaven and . . . the writings of the holy ones" (103:2; see also 93:2). And he in turn hands on books (82:2; 104:12–105:1) to future generations that contain "wisdom which is beyond their thoughts" (82:2).

Though 1 Enoch insists on the heavenly and esoteric character of true wisdom and therefore on the need for a divine revelation of it, it also retains the traditional wisdom idea that creation or nature itself constitutes a kind of revelation. Thus the Astronomical Book (chs 72–82) contains large amounts (especially in the Qumran Aramaic versions) of ancient "scientific" lore pointing toward the rationality of the 364-day solar calendar. And the opening exhortation in 2:1–5:9 is based on looking at how nature – as seen in the heavenly bodies and the earth, the seasons of the year, and the trees – follows the laws of God. It goes on to contrast these "law-abiding" natural phenomena with the transgressions worked by human beings.

The climax and chief content of the heavenly wisdom revealed to Enoch is the restoration of creation at the coming divine visitation. The roots of iniquity were planted by the wicked angels who revealed to humans their evil secrets about weapons, women's seductiveness, and magic (8:1–4). But in the endtime "the roots of iniquity will be cut off" (91:11).

First Enoch contains several apocalyptic scenarios in which wisdom plays a decisive role. In the Ten-Week Apocalypse the decisive transition from past to future involves resurrection and wisdom: "And the righteous will rise from sleep, and wisdom will rise and will be given to them" (91:10). Until then those who are chosen by God and seek to be righteous get plenty of exhortation from 1 Enoch. The style and content of the Epistle of Enoch (chs 91–107) is like the hortatory material in the first part of the Damascus Document and like many of the wisdom instructions found at Qumran. For example, "And now I say to you, my children, love righteousness and walk in it; for the paths of righteousness are worthy of acceptance, but paths of iniquity will quickly be destroyed and vanish" (94:1).

The biblical identifications between the wise and the righteous, and between the fool and the wicked are taken for granted in 1 Enoch. The vindication of the righteous in the endtime will usher in an age of perfect wisdom: "When wisdom is given to the chosen, they will all live, and will not again do wrong" (5:8). And then the righteous "will live in goodness and in righteousness and will walk in eternal light" (92:4).

OTHER RESOURCES

The "wisdom psalms" of the Hebrew Bible are not a sharply defined genre. Some psalms that do not fit elsewhere and have even a few "wisdom" phrases sometimes get put into this category by default. And there is no agreement among scholars as to what belongs on the list of "wisdom psalms."

There is, however, close to universal agreement that Psalm 1 is a wisdom psalm. For understanding Qumran wisdom there are three important points in Psalm 1 (which can be found in other wisdom psalms also). The psalm begins with a "beatitude": "Happy are those who do not follow the advice of the wicked." The beatitude is a typical wisdom form in which the speaker declares someone to be happy or fortunate for some possession or character trait or way of acting. The two kinds of people sketched in Psalm 1 are not so much the wise and the foolish as the righteous and the wicked/sinners. This psalm (and many other biblical texts) emphasizes the moral dimensions and consequences of living according to wisdom. And the source of wisdom is the Torah: "Their delight is in the Law of the Lord, and on his Law they meditate day and night" (Ps 1:2).

The book of Job is a searching examination of the usual sapiential explanations of suffering. There is nothing like it among the Qumran wisdom texts, though it was read at Qumran and was the subject of Aramaic paraphrases or targums. But the poetic interlude in Job 28 on the elusive character of wisdom ("Where shall wisdom be found? And where is the place of understanding?") can help us to grasp an important feature of Qumran wisdom: the need for the revelation of God's wisdom, because true wisdom transcends and eludes human understanding. According to Job 28:23 only God understands the way to wisdom and knows its place. In many of the Qumran texts, there is talk about the "mystery" that has been revealed or is about to be revealed. Unless God had made known his secret wisdom to the community through its teacher(s), the community would be still wandering about in darkness. As it is, through the revelation of the "mystery that is to be/come" the members know what the future holds and how to behave in the present.

Though the Qumran wisdom texts may share a few points of form and content with the book of Qohelet or Ecclesiastes (found at Qumran), what is far more important are their differences. Adopting the persona of the teacher/king (Solomon?), the author whom we call "Qohelet" (the "preacher") puts forth a very personal and idiosyncratic form of wisdom instruction. At Qumran there is nothing like the individual (as well as provocative and entertaining) voice that we hear in Ecclesiastes.

Likewise, the Greek Wisdom of Solomon (not found at Qumran) is important for our purposes mainly as providing a contrasting approach to Jewish wisdom. That work reflects the cosmopolitan atmosphere of Alexandria in Egypt in the first century. Its author, also adopting the persona of Solomon, boldly attempts to put together the traditions of Judaism with the concepts (body and soul anthropology, immortality of the soul, the world soul, the cardinal virtues, and so forth) and methods (allegorical interpretation) of popular Greek philosophy. There is nothing like this at Qumran.

3

BIBLICAL WISDOM TEXTS AND TARGUMS AT QUMRAN

INTRODUCTION

The focus of this book is the previously unknown wisdom writings that have been discovered at Qumran. But this is not the whole story of wisdom at Qumran. Any assessment of the significance of the discovery of the Qumran scrolls would have to give a very high place to the biblical manuscripts. The standard editions of the Hebrew Bible are based largely on manuscripts from around 1000 CE. At Qumran there were found at least fragments of every book in the Hebrew canon of Scripture except Esther. Whether Esther's absence should be attributed to historical accident or to the absence of the divine name in its Hebrew version, can be debated. Indeed, J. T. Milik has argued for a primitive version ("proto-Esther") of Esther in Qumran texts (Milik 1992: 321–99). But the most important point is that we now have access to manuscript evidence for the Hebrew Bible 1,000 or more years earlier than had been available before the discoveries at Qumran.

In content the Qumran biblical manuscripts range from the practically complete (Isaiah) to only a few words or letters. On the whole, the Qumran biblical manuscripts have established the fundamental reliability of the Hebrew textual tradition. In most cases the Qumran manuscripts agree more or less with the biblical manuscripts from around 1000 CE. Or to put it more accurately, those manuscripts stand faithfully in the ancient Jewish textual tradition that is also represented in the Qumran biblical scrolls.

Yet the Hebrew biblical textual tradition at Qumran was not entirely uniform. Indeed, one of the early surprises from the Qumran scrolls was the recognition by scholars that in some instances a Qumran Hebrew text might agree with the Greek Septuagint against the Masoretic tradition (the "standard" Jewish text since the second century CE at least) as well as the Samaritan biblical tradition. In such cases the Septuagint may represent not careless or bad translation but a different Hebrew original. And in some cases the Qumran texts supply that Hebrew original. While establishing the basic reliability of the Hebrew text, the Qumran biblical scrolls at the same time showed that a certain textual diversity regarding the Bible existed at Qumran.

One early explanation of this textual diversity was to postulate the existence of local texts. This hypothesis was put forward most vigorously by Frank M. Cross (1995) and his students. They linked various Qumran biblical texts with the Masoretic, Septuagint, and Samaritan traditions, and assigned them to various locations: Babylon, Alexandria, and Palestine, respectively. Other scholars, principally Emanuel Tov (1992), have contended that the local texts theory oversimplifies the evidence and covers over what was an even more complicated and messy textual situation. Both agree that the so-called Masoretic tradition was one among several at Qumran.

This chapter first surveys the textual evidence for the biblical wisdom books at Qumran. Then it considers the targums (or Aramaic translations/paraphrases) of the book of Job that were found at Qumran.

MANUSCRIPTS OF BIBLICAL WISDOM BOOKS

There are fragments of the books of Proverbs, Ecclesiastes/ Qohelet, Job, and Sirach among the Qumran manuscripts (Nebe 1994: 307–13; Ulrich 1995: 86–107). Canticles (or Song of Songs) is also well represented. But it has nothing to do with the wisdom trajectory that is being pursued in this study, even though it is sometimes classified as a wisdom book. There is nothing from the book of Wisdom. Nor would one expect to find Wisdom among the Qumran scrolls, since it was composed in Greek most likely at Alexandria in the first century BCE and uses the language and concepts of Greek philosophy along with biblical and other Jewish traditions.

The manuscripts designated 4Q102 and 4Q103 contain Hebrew fragments of the book of Proverbs. The column that constitutes 4Q102 supplies Hebrew text from Proverbs 1:27–2:1. 4Q103 contains remnants of Proverbs 14:31–15:8 and 15:19b–31 in two columns, as well as fragments of 13:6b–9b; 14:6–10; and 14:12b, 13b. In both cases the texts are written in "stichs," that is, in sense lines with the two parallel clauses of the verse on the same line. The same arrangement was used in the Masada manuscript of Sirach (see the Appendix). The wisdom texts from Qumran treated here were generally not given this stichic treatment, mainly because they are not as rigidly stichic in their structure as Proverbs and Sirach are.

The book of Ecclesiastes (or Qohelet) is represented by 4Q109 and 4Q110. 4Q109 was published in 1954 by James Muilenberg (1954: 20–28) and has already been incorporated into the standard edition of the Hebrew Bible. It contains text from Ecclesiastes 5:13–17; 6:3–8; and 7:1–2, 4–9, 19–20. Its script is dated to the mid-second century BCE, thus refuting the claims of older scholars about a late second-or first-century BCE origin for the book. There are some variants from the Masoretic text, though none are of extraordinary importance. There is no effort at stichic arrangement. 4Q110 consists of two small fragments that probably belong together. One fragment provides text from Ecclesiastes 1:10–13, and the other from 1:13ff. (perhaps with 1:15 omitted).

Although it contains only a few legible letters spread over three lines, 2Q15 is identified (Baillet et al. 1962: 71) as Job 33:28–30 and said to suppose a Masoretic text type. The Hebrew text of Job is represented in Cave 4 by 4Q99, 4Q100, and 4Q101, respectively. The most extensive manuscript is 4Q99, which supplies text from Job 7:11–13; 15:8–9; 31:14–19; 32:3b, 4; 33:23c(?), 25–30; 34:28–29(?); 35:11(?), 16; and 36:8–37:5. This manuscript is by and large identical with the Masoretic text. 4Q100 consists of four small fragments with text from Job 8:15ff(?); 13:4a; 14:4–6; and 31:21. There is only one minor deviation from the Masoretic text (in 8:15). 4Q101 contains Hebrew text from Job 13:18–20, 23–27; and 14:13–18 (Skehan et al. 1992: 155–57). It is written in the ancient Hebrew script (palaeo-Hebrew) used otherwise only in texts of the Pentateuch. The manuscript is dated between 225 and 150 BCE. The use of the palaeo-Hebrew script may reflect the idea that Job was written before Moses or even by Moses (see b. Baba Batra 14b–15a: "Now on the view that Job lived in the days of Moses . . . "). Indeed, the status of Job implied by the use of palaeo-Hebrew script may be the reason why the targums from Qumran all are on the Pentateuch or Job. The meager textual remains generally agree with the Masoretic text. Far more important than these fragments for understanding the text of Job are the Aramaic targums discussed in the second part of this chapter.

The importance of Sirach 51 for understanding wisdom at Qumran will be made clear in Chapter 4 of this book. The presence of the Hebrew text of Sirach 51:13–19a, 30 in the Cave 11 Psalms Scroll (11Q5) contributes greatly to what evidence there is at Qumran for the female personification of Wisdom. Qumran Cave 2 yielded two small fragments of the Hebrew text of Sirach (2Q18) dated to the second half of the first century BCE. They correspond to Sirach 6:14–15, 20–31. Though only a few letters can be discerned with confidence, these fragments confirm the antiquity of the Hebrew text of Sirach and the basic reliability of the medieval manuscripts from the Cairo Geniza. These texts also appear to have been arranged in stichic form. However, the most important recent discovery of the Hebrew text of Sirach came not from Qumran but rather from Masada (see the Appendix).

The manuscripts of the biblical wisdom books at Qumran are consistent with what has already been said about the other (and much more extensive) biblical manuscripts. They provide the oldest textual evidence by far for the biblical wisdom books (especially 4Q101 and 4Q109). They confirm the basic reliability of the Hebrew textual tradition now represented by the Masoretic text. With their variant readings they also illustrate the fluidity of the Hebrew textual tradition up to the late first century CE. The stichic arrangement of parts of Proverbs and Sirach shows that scribes in antiquity were sensitive to the parallelism of thought and expression that is so characteristic of the biblical wisdom books, and were prepared to use up precious space on their manuscripts to bring it out.

The biblical wisdom manuscripts from Qumran do not shed much light on the debate about local texts. They are simply too fragmentary to help much. To say that they agree with the Masoretic text in this case means simply that the Masoretic text provides the only real parallel evidence we have, and not that the manuscripts necessarily represent that distinctive branch of the Hebrew biblical textual tradition.

Likewise, the presence of fragments of Sirach at Qumran (2Q18 and 11Q5) neither proves nor disproves its canonical status there. In fact, it is difficult to ascertain which books (if any) were regarded as canonical at Qumran or whether canonical is a meaningful term to use with reference to the Qumran community. Some of the canonical books are quoted as authoritative, form the basis of other

17

writings, and serve as the starting point for commentaries (Pesharim). But there is no list of canonical books at Qumran, nor is there generally any material difference between canonical and non-canonical manuscripts except perhaps in the occasional use of the palaeo-Hebrew script for the Pentateuch and Job.

THE TARGUMS OF JOB

A targum is an Aramaic translation of a Hebrew biblical text. For Jewish communities in the eastern Diaspora and even in the Land of Israel such renderings were used in liturgical and perhaps educational settings. Presumably there was need for such aids when and where the knowledge of biblical Hebrew had grown weak. Some of the rabbinic targums are fairly straightforward translations, whereas others are so expansive as to constitute paraphrases or even short anthologies of interpretive traditions related to specific biblical verses.

There are longstanding debates about the antiquity of the rabbinic targums and about the validity of their use as parallels in interpreting New Testament and early Jewish texts. The discovery of two Targums of Job at Qumran – 4Q Targum of Job (4Q157) and 11Q Targum of Job (11Q10) – at least established the existence of the targum as a literary genre in the first century, although it did not resolve the debates about the age of the rabbinic targums or their value in providing parallels. The existence of an ancient Aramaic version of Job is attested by a talmudic story about Rabbi Gamaliel (*t. Shabbat* 13:2: "R. Halafta once visited Rabban Gamaliel . . . and in his hand was a targum scroll of Job, and he was reading in it") and by Job 42:17b in the Septuagint version. But there is no way to be sure whether there is any connection between these references and the Qumran Targums of Job.

The Cave 4 Targum of Job (4Q157) provides fragments of an Aramaic version of Job 3:5–9 (col. i) and 4:16–5:4 (col. ii) (Milik 1977: 90). The script of the manuscript is dated to the mid-first century CE, though the Targum of course may have been composed much earlier. The Aramaic text (where it can be read) is close to the Hebrew. It may well represent the same work as appears in the Cave 11 Targum of Job (11Q10). But since the early chapters of Job are missing from the Cave 11 manuscript, there is no way to be certain about this.

The Cave 11 Targum of Job (11Q10) is far more extensive and

important (van der Ploeg and van der Woude 1971). It consists of thirty-eight columns, which contain an Aramaic version of much of Job 17:14 through 42:11. The early part of the book has been lost. The abrupt ending may be intentional rather than accidental (see the second text discussed below). The script of the manuscript is dated to the early first century CE. The language, however, suggests an earlier date of composition – between the final redaction of Daniel and the composition of the Genesis Apocryphon, about 100 BCE (Jongeling 1972: 191–97; Weiss 1974: 13–18).

The Hebrew text underlying the Targum is fairly close to that which is preserved in the Masoretic text. The language of Job is notoriously difficult, and 11Q Targum of Job provides, according to Michael Sokoloff (1974: 8) "a more readable and internally consistent text" than the Masoretic text does. The Targum was most likely made because readers found the Hebrew so hard and needed help in understanding the text (Fitzmyer 1974: 503–24; 1977: 161–82).

There is nothing in the text of 11Q10 that links it directly to Qumran beyond the fact that it was discovered there. It was perhaps only part of the library collection and shows no "sectarian" characteristics. This seems to have been the case with most or all of the Aramaic texts found at Qumran. Conversely, no "sectarian" document was written in Aramaic. The Targum of Job is not demonstrably representative of the Qumran sect or even of the wider movement that is reflected in some of the Qumran wisdom texts. On the other hand, there is no real connection between the Qumran Cave 11 Targum of Job and the later rabbinic Targum of Job. The language and method of translation are very different.

The two texts that are translated and analyzed below – Job 38:3–13 (= 11QtgJob xxx) and Job 42:9–11 (= 11QtgJob xxxviii 2–5) – illustrate the nature and the distinctive contributions of this Qumran targum. Where the Aramaic text agrees with the Masoretic text, the translation appears in Roman type. Where it diverges, it appears in italics. The double number refers to the biblical chapter and verse (38:3), and the single number refers to the line in the column of the Qumran manuscript (xxx 1).

TEXT 1: JOB 38:3–13 = 11QtgJOB xxx 1–10

Text

38:3/xxx 1 Now gird [your] loin[s] like a man, [and let me] ask you. *Give me an answer. 38:4/2* Where were you *when I made* the earth? Tell *me* if you know wisdom. *38:5/3* Who set its measurements if you know? Who stretched over it the line? *38:6 Or 4* on what are its foundations laid? Or who erected its cornerstone, *38:7* while *5* the morning stars *shone* all at once and all the *angels* of God cried out *all at once?*

38:8/6 Is it you who shut in the sea with doors when it came gushing from the womb *of the deep 7* to surge forth *38:9* with the donning of clouds for its [gar]ment and thick darkness for its swaddling clothes? *38:10 Is it you who set 8* for it boundaries and b[olts and doo]rs? *38:11* And *[have you answered] and said*: "Up to this point! *9 And you shall not again [come further* with your proud w]aves"? *38:12* Have you in your days appointed *10* [the morning and shown the dawn its place, *38:13* to take hold of the] skirt[s of the] earth] . . . ?

Exposition

This passage marks the beginning of God's speech to Job from the whirlwind. After Job's relentless questioning of his friends and of God that constitutes most of the biblical book, God turns the tables on Job and makes some brutal inquiries of him.

Most of the text of Job 38:3–13 in column xxx of 11Qtg Job is a straightforward rendering of the Hebrew version as we know it. The minor deviations from the Hebrew can be explained in one of several ways: the use of a slightly different Hebrew original, the exigencies of Aramaic idiom, and the interpretative dimension inherent in any translation (especially of a text as difficult as the Hebrew Job is).

Two points, however, demand particular attention: the painting over of mythological imagery in Job 38:7, and the change in the rhetorical pattern of God's questions in Job 38:8, 10, 11.

The Hebrew text of Job 38:7 portrays the morning stars as "singing" and says that the "sons of God" cried out. The scene is the familiar ancient Near Eastern and biblical picture of the heavenly court. In its Israelite version the Lord presides over a court filled with other heavenly beings (see Job 1). The first image in Job 38:7

personifies the morning stars and makes them capable of "singing." The targumist destroys the personification by having the stars perform only their natural function of "shining." The second image in Job 38:7 has the "sons" of God crying out. The targumist identifies the "sons" with the angels – heavenly beings but clearly subordinate in nature to the creator God in Jewish theology. This tendency to protect the uniqueness and transcendence of Israel's God even by "correcting" or at least "interpreting" the Hebrew biblical text is a characteristic feature in the later rabbinic targums. Here we have a first-century example of that tendency.

The second major change in this column of the Targum of Job comes in the rhetorical pattern used in the questions posed by God in Job 38:8, 10, 11. The Hebrew text continues the pattern begun in Job 38:5 ("Who . . . ?") with statements that expect the response "God, not you Job." In the Aramaic version, however, Job is addressed directly: "Is it you who shut in . . . ? Is it you who set . . . ? And have you answered and said . . . ?" These questions expect the response "Not you Job, but God." By recasting the biblical statements in the second person singular and making them into the form of rhetorical questions asked directly of Job, the targumist has produced an unbroken succession of rhetorical questions from Job 38:4 through 38:12 (a pattern that is interrupted in the Masoretic text). Whether this difference reflects a variant Hebrew original or the literary sensitivity of the targumist cannot be determined.

TEXT 2: JOB 42:9–11 = 11QtgJOB xxxviii 1–8

Text

42:9/xxxviii 2 And *God listened to the voice of Job, and He forgave 3 them their sins on account of him. 42:10 And God turned to Job in mercy 4 and gave to him* twice as much as all that he had before. *42:11* And there came to *5 Job all his friends* and all his brothers and all his acquaintances, and they ate *6* bread with him in his house. And they consoled him for all the misfortune that *7 God* brought upon him. And they gave to him, each one a *ewe lamb 8* and each a ring of gold.

21

Exposition

While the first thirty-seven columns of 11Q Targum of Job stay fairly close to what has become the traditional Hebrew text of the book, the final column shows some striking differences. The rendering of Job 42:9–10a ("God listened . . . turned to Job in mercy") is more paraphrase than direct translation, though the content can be traced to the Hebrew of Job 42:10 ("when he had prayed for his friends"). Note that here as elsewhere in the Targum of Job there is no effort to indicate the use of the special divine name YHWH that is characteristic of this part of the Hebrew text of Job.

The Qumran Targum of Job 42:11 is noteworthy first of all for the list of those invited to Job's feast: "all his friends and all his brothers and all his acquaintances." The Masoretic text has "all his brothers and all his sisters and all his acquaintances." Why the targumist omitted "all his sisters" and changed the order is not clear. There could have been a different Hebrew original. Or perhaps some trace of misogynism or a suggestion about celibacy might be in the background. Secondly, where the Hebrew of Job 42:11 has two verbs ("they showed him sympathy and consoled him"), the Targum has only one ("they consoled him"). Finally, the Hebrew text contains a mysterious word *qĕsîtâ* among the gifts brought to Job. Modern commentators give various interpretations ranging from the vague "something valuable" to the very specific ("a weight of silver used in financial transactions," see Gen 33:19). The targumist offers the clear (though not necessarily correct) translation "ewe lamb."

The text of the book of Job in the Cave 11 Targum breaks off at 42:11 – in the middle of a line, with still some empty space at the bottom of the column and a following column that is entirely blank. Thus it lacks Job 42:12–17 and the expanded epilogue in the Septuagint version. It would appear that the Hebrew text on which 11Q Targum of Job was based ended at 42:11 and lacked 42:12–17 entirely.

4

WISDOM IN THE PSALMS SCROLL FROM CAVE 11

INTRODUCTION

The great Psalms Scroll from Qumran Cave 11 (Sanders 1965, 1967) designated as 11Q Ps[a] or 11Q5 contains all or part of over forty canonical psalms (from Psalms 101 to 150) as well as eight additional works – four known previously, and four "new" works. The four known previously are Psalms 151, 154, and 155, as well as Sirach 51:13–19, 30. The Psalms, known from the Syriac biblical tradition, reflect Palestinian Hebrew sources, and so it is not entirely surprising to find the Hebrew originals at Qumran. The four "new" works are entitled the "Plea for Deliverance," "Apostrophe to Zion," "Hymn to the Creator," and a prose summary of David's compositions (García Martínez 1994: 304–9; Vermes 1995: 238–43). The script in which the manuscript is written suggests a date in the first century CE, though of course the original composition (of which this manuscript was a copy) may have been much older.

For those interested in the textual criticism of the Psalms this scroll provides important manuscript evidence that is 1,000 years earlier than what had been previously available. One scholar (Chyutin: 1994: 367–95) finds in the order of the Psalms in 11Q5 a deliberate support for the solar calendar of 364 days over and against the lunar calendar of 354 days that he discerns behind the traditional order of the Psalms in what has become the canonical book.

The major problem posed by the Cave 11 Psalms Scroll is the nature and status of the work. The order of the Psalms is not our familiar canonical order, and the scroll contains several noncanonical works. One can explain this fact in several ways. Perhaps our canonical order and scope were not set when this work was assembled. Or perhaps the Qumran scroll provides evidence for an alternative Psalter. Or perhaps this scroll may be simply a non-official hymnbook that interspersed biblical and nonbiblical works, much as hymnbooks today do.

A second problem is the nature of the eight nonbiblical texts: Are they "sectarian?" There is not much in these texts that would clearly identify them with Qumran works judged to be sectarian (Community Rule, Thanksgiving Hymns, Habakkuk Pesher, etc.). And yet the content of some (if not all of these works) includes material that would have been at home or even welcomed by the Qumran sectarians.

On both these issues, a minimalist approach is probably best. The Cave 11 Psalms Scroll is at least a hymnbook copied and probably used by the Qumran sectarians. And the nonbiblical material in it was at least regarded as acceptable and even significant by the Qumran sectarians. Indeed, some of the sapiential material may have been especially appropriate to their situations. What follows focuses on those nonbiblical texts in the Cave 11 Psalms Scroll (11Q5) that can contribute to our appreciation of wisdom at Qumran.

DAVID'S COMPOSITIONS (11Q5 xxvii 2–11)

The prose summary of David's compositions toward the end of the scroll attributes 4,050 works to David: 3,600 psalms, as well as 364 songs for the daily offering, 52 for the Sabbath offerings, and 30 for the New Moons and other festivals (= 446), and 4 songs for the "stricken." What is important for the study of wisdom at Qumran is how David is described just before the list of his alleged compositions: "wise and brilliant like the light of the sun; and a scribe, intelligent and perfect in all his ways before God and men." David the prolific psalmist was also a model sage!

Yet the origin of David's wisdom was not his innate cleverness or experience. Rather, "the Lord gave him a discerning and brilliant spirit." Indeed, David the sage who wrote so many psalms and songs was also a prophet: "All these he spoke through prophecy which was given him from before the Most High." This understanding of David as a prophet is important for viewing the Psalms as prophecies both at Qumran (and so they can receive the "pesher" treatment) and in the New Testament (and so they can be "fulfilled" by Jesus). The biblical categories of psalmist, sage, and prophet coalesce in the figure of David. And the source of his wisdom is divine revelation.

HYMN TO THE CREATOR (11Q5 xxvi 9–15)

Text

9 Great and holy is the Lord, the holiest for every generation. Before Him splendor *10* goes, and after Him abundance of many waters. Lovingkindness and truth are round about Him; truth *11* and justice and righteousness are the foundation of His throne.

He separates light from darkness; He establishes the dawn by the knowledge of *12* His heart. When all His angels saw (it), they sang aloud, for He showed them what they had not known. *13* He crowns the mountains with fruit, good food for every living being.

Blessed be He who makes *14* the earth by His power, who establishes the world by His wisdom. By His understanding He stretched out the heavens, and He brought forth *15* [wind] from [His store]houses. [Lightning for the ra]in He made, and brought up mi[sts from] the end of [the earth].

Exposition

The Hymn to the Creator is sapiential in the sense that it celebrates God's wisdom and understanding made manifest in creation. What exists of the hymn (and it may have been longer) first describes the great and holy Lord in His heavenly court. Then in talking about creation it introduces the theme of God's wisdom: "He establishes the dawn by the knowledge of His heart." Indeed, it portrays creation as a display or show for the angels: "He showed them what they had not known." The third part is a blessing: "Blessed be He who makes the earth by His power. . . ." The reason why God is blessed is the wisdom that He showed in creation: "who establishes the world by His wisdom. By His understanding He stretched out the heavens. . . ." The language here is familiar from Jeremiah 10:12–13; 51:15–16; and Psalm 135:7. The idea of wisdom as God's agent in creation is developed at great length, of course, in Proverbs 8:22–31 and related texts. The occurrences of the motif in the

25

Hymn to the Creator at least establish a link between divine wisdom and creation. They also point toward and prepare for fuller personifications of Wisdom and Folly.

PSALM 154 (11Q5 xviii 1–16)

Text

1 . . . assemble together to make known His saving power, and do not be slow *2* to make known His power and His majesty *3* to all the simple.

For wisdom is given to make known the glory of the Lord, and to recount *4* the greatness of His deeds she has been made known to humans, to make known to the simple His power, *5* to make those lacking heart (understand) about His greatness, those far from her gates, *6* those straying from her entrances.

For the Most High, He is Lord *7* of Jacob, and His majesty is over all His works. And one who glorifies the Most High *8* He accepts as one who brings a meal offering, as one who offers he-goats and calves, *9* as one who fattens the altar with many holocausts, as sweet-smelling incense from the hand *10* of the righteous.

From the gates of the righteous her voice is heard, and from the assembly of the pious *11* her song. When they eat in fullness, she is mentioned; and when they drink in community *12* together, their meditation is on the Law of the Most High, their words to make known His power. *13* How far from the wicked is her word, from all the insolent is knowledge of her.

Behold *14* the eyes of the Lord upon the good are compassionate, and upon those who glorify Him He increases His mercy. *15* From an evil time He will deliver their souls [. . .] redeem the humble from the hand [of the wicked].

Exposition

The Cave 11 Psalms Scroll contains most of the Hebrew text of a psalm that had been previously known in Syriac and called Psalm 154. Though verses 1–2 and most of verses 18–20 of Psalm 154 are missing because the manuscript is damaged, their Hebrew text can be easily reconstructed from the Syriac (a cognate Semitic-language version).

The full text of Psalm 154 begins with a call to the communal praise of God expressed in a series of plural imperatives: "Glorify God . . . proclaim . . . glorify . . . recount . . . join your souls . . . assemble . . . be not slow." The main part of Psalm 154 consists of four stanzas – two of which (first and third) concern wisdom, and the other two (second and fourth) deal with the sacrifice of praise and God's mercy toward Israel. The speaker summons those being addressed (the "simple") to join themselves to the "good" and the "perfect" and to avoid the "wicked" and "insolent."

The first wisdom stanza (lines 3–6 = verses 5–8) gives the reason ("for . . .") why the "simple" should join the "good" in the communal praise of God: "For wisdom is given to make known the glory of the Lord, and to recount the greatness of His deeds she has been made known to humans." Wisdom is a gift from God, not a human achievement. Wisdom's purpose is theological – to make known God's glory. Its possession is communal, not individual. The wisdom given by God has the power to bring the "simple" and those without understanding ("lacking heart") to God. The description of such persons as "far from her gates" and "straying from her entrances" evokes the language of Proverbs 8–9. They too can become wise, unlike the wicked and insolent.

The second wisdom stanza of Psalm 154 (lines 10–13 = verses 12–15) celebrates the wisdom community: "From the gates of the righteous her voice is heard, and from the assembly of the pious her song." The setting recalls the repeated opening invitations to join in the communal praise of God. The "her" is wisdom. The Hebrew noun *ḥokmâ* is feminine in gender, and thus takes feminine pronouns. The celebration of wisdom extends even to the community's meals: "When they eat in fullness, she is mentioned; and when they drink in community together, their meditation is on the Law of the Most High." This stanza contains three important motifs that recur in other Qumran wisdom texts: the wisdom community, the (feminine) personification of wisdom, and the association between wisdom and the Law of the Most High.

The appearance of these three motifs in turn raises some questions. (1) Was Psalm 154 a Qumran sectarian composition? Probably not. The language is generic and could apply to many religious communities (even today!). Nevertheless, what is said in Psalm 154 would have been perfectly appropriate to the Qumran sectarians – an impression strengthened by its theology of the "sacrifice of praise" as the equivalent of temple sacrifices, and its hopes for a

27

purified and renewed Mount Zion. (2) How strongly is Wisdom personified? There are references to Wisdom's gates and entrances, her voice and song, and her word. But these feminine possessive pronouns flow naturally from the Hebrew feminine noun *ḥokmâ* ("wisdom"), and so it is hard to discern just how sharply Wisdom is being personified. (3) How is wisdom related to the Torah – the Law of the Most High? This identification is made most dramatically in Sirach 24, especially in 24:23: "All this (Wisdom) is the book of the covenant of the Most High God, the law that Moses commanded us." In Psalm 154 the Law is at least one kind of wisdom, one component of what constitutes the fullness of wisdom. In fact, Ben Sira himself did not see a perfect equation between Wisdom and Torah. Otherwise, he would not have conducted a wisdom school or written a wisdom book (rather than simply repeating the Torah). Instead, he sought to integrate the legal, prophetic, and historical strands of Israel's tradition with the wisdom traditions of Israel and the ancient Near East.

SIRACH 51:13–19, 30 (11Q5 xxi 11–17; xxii 1)

The book of Sirach (also known as Ecclesiasticus in its Greek version and Ben Sira in its Hebrew version; see the Appendix on the Hebrew Ben Sira text from Masada) ends with an autobiographical poem on the search for wisdom. Other small fragments of Sirach have been found at Qumran (2Q18), and so we should not be entirely surprised to find this poem on the Cave 11 Psalms Scroll (Lehmann 1983: 239–51). And yet there is a debate about whether this "autobiographical poem" contained in Sirach 51 really came from Ben Sira and belonged to his wisdom book. The poem in Sirach first describes the speaker's search for and discovery of wisdom (51:18–22). The second part (51:23–30) is an invitation for students to join the speaker's school.

It is conceivable that such a poem was originally independent (whether from Ben Sira or someone else) and later attached to the book of Sirach because it was so appropriate (and independently included in the Cave 11 Psalms Scroll text). On the other hand, if Ben Sira did not write the poem, he should have done so, because it captures so well the spirit of his entire book. It is not crucial for our purposes to decide this debate. What is important is that in Sirach 51:13–30 we have evidence at Qumran for the vivid personification of Wisdom as a female figure.

Only part (Sirach 51:13–19) of the first half of the autobiographical poem is preserved in column xxi of the Cave 11 Psalms Scroll. The presence of the second half (Sirach 51:23–30) is indicated by the last words of verse 30 in the beginning of column xxii. The full text of the Greek version can be found in the various modern Bible translations.

What is preserved of the first part tells about a young man's search for Wisdom as a female figure (and her search for him). The Qumran Hebrew version differs somewhat from the Greek and medieval Hebrew versions. The first editor of the Qumran text, James A. Sanders (1965), regarded its imagery as highly erotic and translated it accordingly. There is certainly a sexual component to the poem (as in Proverbs 8–9; Sirach 15:1–8; and Wisdom 8:2–21). And indeed it is possible to construe the Hebrew text in a more erotic fashion than the Greek allows (which spiritualizes the poem with references to prayer and the temple in 51:13–14). But perhaps it is still not as graphic as Sanders maintains (Deutsch 1982: 400–9; Muraoka 1979: 166–78). What follows are my own (less erotic) translations.

The first part (Sirach 51:13–17) according to the Cave 11 text describes the speaker's quest for Wisdom:

> When I was a young man before I travelled, I sought her. She came to me in her beauty (or, search), and unto the end I will search for her. As a blossom drops in the ripening of grapes, making glad the heart, so my foot walked on the straight path, for from my youth I knew her. I inclined my ear a little, and much instruction I found. And progress (or, a nurse) she was for me, and to my teacher I give my glory.

Even in this minimally erotic translation, it is clear that a young man seeks out Lady Wisdom, and that the search is in fact a mutual one (for she revealed herself to him). Both figures ("I" and "she") are lively and quite concrete characters. The concern for Wisdom in a poetic or even liturgical/cultic text such as Sirach 51:13–30 may suggest a priestly perspective (common in many "sectarian" texts from Qumran) that seeks to make wisdom part of revelation/ prophecy, whereas in other genres wisdom maintains its traditional integrity based on human experience. This observation could apply equally to the "priestly" community at Qumran and to Ben Sira who was a great supporter of the Jerusalem Temple and its priesthood.

Only the beginning (= Sirach 51:18–19) of the speaker's resolve to live by Wisdom is preserved. The speaker's true and pure love for Wisdom has taken over his whole life:

> I resolved and delighted in her, and I was zealous for good, and I shall not turn back. I inflamed my soul for her, and my face I did not turn away. I stirred my soul for her, and on the heights I will not waver. My hands I opened . . . and from her shrewdness I came to know. My palms I cleansed. . . .

What cannot be made clear in any English translation is the fact that this poem is an acrostic; that is, each line begins with a new letter of the Hebrew alphabet according to the Hebrew alphabetical order. This device, which appears also in the Hebrew Bible (see especially Proverbs 31 and Psalm 119) conveys a sense of fullness and orderliness to the content – in this case the search for and discovery of Lady Wisdom as a female personal figure.

The evidence from the Cave 11 Psalms Scroll has to be used with caution in referring to the Qumran community. It is not a clearly "sectarian" document (though the prose summary of David's compositions does assume a solar, 364-day calendar – a characteristic concern of sectarian texts). At the very least, however, it does give us some preliminary ideas and motifs about wisdom that were present at Qumran: David the psalmist as a sage and prophet; wisdom as God's agent in creation; glorifying God as the purpose of wisdom, and the ideal of the wisdom community; and Wisdom as a female figure for whom those who wish to be wise should search and by whom they might live.

5

FOLLY AND WISDOM IN 4Q184–185

INTRODUCTION

The manuscripts from Qumran Cave 4 that were edited by John M. Allegro (1968) included two important (though fragmentary) wisdom texts. One text (4Q184) is a somewhat lurid description of Lady Folly – a personification of foolishness as a female figure well known from the early chapters of Proverbs. The text is clearly intended to warn those seeking righteousness against the seductions of folly and sin. The second text (4Q185) is part of a wisdom instruction in which an experienced and wise sage warns his listeners against choosing the way of foolishness and urges them instead to follow the way of wisdom and righteousness. Allegro's editions of these texts need to be supplemented and corrected by the long review article written by John Strugnell (1970: 163–276). Indeed, there are more pages in Strugnell's review article than in Allegro's edition!

LADY FOLLY (4Q184 1)

Text

1 [. . .] she utters folly [. . .] for perversities she is always searching. She sharpens the words of her mouth, *2* and she imparts mockery so as to lead people astray with evil nonsense. Her heart is set up as a snare, and her kidneys as nets; her eyes are defiled *3* with iniquity; her hands descend to the pit; her feet go down to work wickedness and to walk in the guilt of transgression. *4* [Her . . .] are foundations of darkness; many sins are in her skirts. Her [. . .] are darkness of night, and her garments [. . .] *5* her clothes are shadows of twilight, and her

31

ornaments are plagues of corruption. Her beds are couches of corruption *6* [. . .] depths of the pit, her lodgings are beds of darkness. In the deep of night are her tents; in the foundations of gloom *7* she sets up her dwelling, and she inhabits the tents of silence. Amid everlasting fire is her inheritance, not among all those *8* who shine brightly.

She is the beginning of all the ways of iniquity. Alas, there shall be ruin to all who possess her, and destruction to all *9* who take hold of her. For her ways are ways of death, and her paths are roads of sin; her tracks lead astray *10* to iniquity, and her paths to the guilt of transgression. Her gates are gates of death; at the entrance of her house Sheol stands. *11* All [who enter her] shall not return, and all who inherit her will go down to the pit.

She lies in ambush in secret places [. . . *12* . . .]. In the city squares she displays herself, and in town gates she sets herself up, and there is none to interrupt *13* . . . from her perpetual fornication. Her eyes look here and there, and she raises her eyelids naughtily to look at the righteous *14* man to overtake him, and at the important man to trip him up, at upright men to pervert their way, and at the righteous elect *15* to keep them from the commandment, at the firmly established to bring them down wantonly, and those who walk in uprightness to change the statute, to cause *16* the humble to transgress from God, and to turn their steps from the ways of righteousness, to bring insolence to their heart [. . .] so they do not persist *17* in the righteous paths, to lead people astray in the ways of the pit, and to seduce with flatteries the sons of men.

Exposition

Fragment 1 of 4Q184 (Allegro 1968: 82–85; Strugnell 1970: 263–68) contains a poem variously known as the "Wiles of the Wicked Woman" (Allegro 1964: 53–55) and the "Seductress" (Vermes 1995: 273). It is a very negative description of "Lady Folly" in the tradition of and in dependence on Proverbs 2, 5, 7, and 9. In the biblical wisdom tradition, Lady Folly is the antithesis of Lady Wisdom. Portrayed as a prostitute and an adulteress, Lady Folly has the capacity to draw the unwitting or simple away from the path of righteousness and thus to lead them to death (moral and physical). Much of Israelite wisdom literature (see also Sirach) is devoted to instructions from the experienced sage warning his young male students against the attractions of Lady Folly.

The image of Folly as the "loose woman" was part of the Israelite wisdom tradition long before the poem contained in fragment 1 of 4Q184 was composed. It is difficult to know how seriously and how vividly the sexual imagery was intended by the writers and was received by the readers (Baumgarten 1991: 133–43; Broshi 1983: 54–56; Burgmann 1974: 323–59; Gazov-Ginzberg 1967: 279–85; Moore 1981: 505–19). The poem surely originated in a male environment. The life-setting is the instruction of male pupils by the wise male teacher. There may be an element of the sublimation of sexual fantasies, a kind of "holy" titillation. But no one can be sure how strong it was. To use this poem as proof of the alleged misogynism or gynophobia of the Essenes goes far beyond the evidence of what in the last analysis is a fairly conventional portrayal of Lady Folly. Allegorical interpretations of Lady Folly as Rome or Simon the Maccabee have no textual foundation at all.

The first part of what survives of the poem (García Martínez 1994: 379–80; Vermes 1995: 273–74) describes how Lady Folly leads people astray by means of the parts of her body, her clothes, and her dwelling place, respectively. The various parts of her body are instruments of wickedness and death: "her heart is set up as a snare, and her kidneys as nets; her eyes are defiled with iniquity; her hands descend to the pit; her feet go down to work wickedness and to walk in the guilt of transgression." Her clothes are full of darkness and sin: "Her clothes are shadows of twilight, and her ornaments are plagues of corruption." Where she dwells is a place of corruption and darkness: "Her beds are couches of corruption . . . her lodgings are beds of darkness."

The last couplet of this first section introduces the theme of the fate of Lady Folly and those who are seduced by her: "Amid everlasting fire is her inheritance, not among all those who shine brightly." Those who shine brightly are presumably the stars or the angels – the kind of imagery used in Daniel 12:3 to describe the immortality to be enjoyed by the righteous at the resurrection from the dead. The everlasting fire is on the other hand the abode of the wicked as in Matthew 25:41: "You that are accursed, depart from me into the eternal fire prepared for the devil and his angels." In this respect – the theme of the eternal rewards for following Lady Wisdom and the eternal punishment for following Lady Folly, the Qumran text goes beyond what appears in its biblical model, Proverbs 1–9.

The second part of the poem describes the ways and the house of Lady Folly. The key to understanding who is being described appears at the start of the section: "She is the beginning of all the ways of iniquity." This is a play on the description of Wisdom in Job 40:19: "It is the beginning of all the ways of God." For Wisdom as the beginning of God's ways and works, see also Proverbs 8:22: "The Lord created me at the beginning of his work, the first of his acts of long ago." Lady Wisdom finds her evil opposite in Lady Folly.

The ways of Lady Folly are "ways of death . . . roads of sin . . . to iniquity and . . . guilt of transgression." The imagery is based on Proverbs 2:18–19; 5:5–6; and 7:25–26, which emphasize sin and death as the result of following the ways of Lady Folly. Those who enter the house of Lady Folly (see Proverbs 5:8; 9:13–18) will descend to the "pit" and never return, because "her gates are gates of death."

The third part of the poem describes the guile and seductiveness of Lady Folly: "She lies in ambush in secret places [. . .]. In the city squares she displays herself, and in town gates she sets herself up." This portrayal of Lady Folly as a street prostitute echoes what is found in Proverbs 5:3–14; 7:5–23; and 9:14–17. What is distinctive with respect to the poem's biblical model is the nature of Lady Folly's victims. Whereas in Proverbs 1–9 the potential victims are the simple and foolish (the unwise), here they are the righteous: "She raises her eyelids naughtily to look at the righteous man to overtake him, and at the important man to trip him up, at upright men to pervert their way, and at the righteous elect to keep them from the commandment, at the firmly established to bring them down wantonly, and those who walk in uprightness to change the statute."

The emphasis is on morality, not merely wisdom (though the two cannot be separated). The words "commandment" and "statute" could suggest a relation to observance of the Torah or even of the movement's rules. If this text is not clearly "sectarian," at least its content and terminology would have appealed to and have been readily appropriated by the Qumran sectarians. As can be seen from Hodayot and the Community Rule, the Qumran sectarians differentiated themselves sharply as the righteous from the unrighteous and wicked.

The poem about Lady Folly in 4Q184 is manifestly based upon the "Folly" passages scattered throughout Proverbs 1–9. By re-using the language of Proverbs 1–9 and concentrating or focusing only on Lady Folly, the poem has created a harshly negative portrait that is intended to warn the readers against the enticements of Lady Folly. The readers have to make a choice between the way of Wisdom and the way of Folly. The intellectual presupposition of the text is the dualism of the "two ways" found in Proverbs and in the Qumran sectarian writings (the classic example of which is Community Rule iii 13–iv 26). The ways in which the potential victims of Lady Folly ("upright men . . . righteous elect . . . those who walk in uprightness . . . the humble") are described would have made the text especially meaningful to those who regarded themselves as following the path of righteousness in the "covenant of grace" and the "community of God."

WISDOM INSTRUCTION (4Q185 1–2)

Text

[4. . .] pure and holy [. . . 5 . . .] His and according to His wrath [. . . 6 . . .] and unto ten times [. . . 7 . . .] and no strength to stand before her, and none to support 8 the indignation [of her wrath . . .]. And who can endure to stand before His angels? For with a flaming 9 fire they will judge [. . .] of His spirits.

And you, sons of men, woe to you; for behold 10 like grass he sprouts from his ground and his goodliness flowers like a blossom. His wind blows on it, 11 and its herbage dries up, and its blossom the wind bears away unto [. . .] so that it passes [away like a name that pe]rishes, 12 and it is no more found for it is but wind. . . . They will seek him and will not find him, and there is no hope. 13 And he – his days are like a shadow over the l[and].

And now listen please, O my people, and pay attention 14 to me, you simple ones, and draw wisdom from the might of God, and remember the marvels He did 15 in Egypt, and His signs in [the land of Ham]; and let your heart tremble before His dread ii 1 and do His good pleasure [. . .] your souls according to his good mercies. Seek out for yourselves a way 2 to life, a highway [. . .] a remnant for your children after you. And why do you give up 3 your soul to vanity [. . .] judgment?

Listen to me, O my sons, and do not rebel against the words of the Lord. *4* Do not walk in [. . . but in the way He laid down for Ja]cob, and in the path He appointed for Isaac. Is not one *5* day in His house better than [. . .] to fear Him not to be afflicted by fear or the fowler's snare *6* [. . .] to be separated from His angels, for there is no darkness *7* nor gloom [. . . His good pl]easure and His knowledge. And you, *8* what can you understand [. . .] before Him will go forth evil to every people.

Happy is the man to whom she has been given *9* thus [. . .] and let not the wicked boast, saying: "She has not been given *10* to me, nor [has she been measured out to me" . . . for God gave her] to Israel, and with a good measure He measures her out, and all His people He will redeem *11* and He will slay those who hate His wisdom [. . .] He destroys [. . . nor] let those who glory in themselves say: "Thus have we found her." Seek her *12* and find her and hold fast to her and get her as an inheritance. With her is length of days and fatness of bone and joy of heart. *13* Her youth will multiply mercies for him and salvation [. . .].

Happy is the man who does it and does not play tricks against her, nor with [a spirit] *14* of deceit seeks her, nor holds fast to her with flatteries. As she is given to his fathers, so he will inherit her, and [hold fast] to her *15* with all the power of his strength and with all his immeasurable [might], and he will give her as an inheritance to his offspring. I know how to labor at doing good *iii 1* for her, for . . . .

Exposition

Fragments 1 and 2 of 4Q185 (Allegro 1968: 85–87; Strugnell 1970: 269–73) constitute two columns of a wisdom instruction. The script can be dated to the mid- or late first century BCE, and so the work is at least as old as that. Fifteen lines of each column are preserved, but there is only one complete line (4Q185 1 i 12), which itself contains a deliberate blank space (*vacat*) of about five letter spaces. The best preserved material runs from column i, line 9 to the end of column ii. Even there (especially in column ii, lines 1–11), there are large gaps (indicated by square brackets).

Despite the fragmentary character of the manuscript, we can say something about the work with a reasonable degree of confidence

(Lichtenberger 1978: 151–62; Tobin 1990: 145–52). It appears to be part of a wisdom instruction. The speaker is a sage, someone who claims to know about the past, present, and future. Those who are addressed are called variously "sons of men," "my people," "you simple ones," and "my sons." The speaker uses the literary forms of wisdom instructions: calls to pay attention, commands and prohibitions, reasons why the commands should be obeyed ("for . . . "), and beatitudes ("happy is the man who . . . ").

With such a fragmentary text it is of course difficult to be certain about its literary structure and content. And the one certain fact is that we have only part of the work! But the surviving text (García Martínez 1994: 380–82; Vermes 1995: 275–76) nevertheless provides some clues. The first part contains three calls to pay attention: "And you, sons of men . . . now listen please, O my people and pay attention to me, you simple ones. . . . Listen to me, O my sons." Each call introduces a unit of instruction. The second part features two beatitudes ("happy is the man who . . . "). These external literary (and traditionally sapiential) devices can help to make sense out of the text as we have it.

The first complete unit of instruction (i 9–13) is a warning ("woe to you!") to the "sons of men." The combination of "woes" and "beatitudes" also appears in Luke 6:20–26 and Matthew 5:3–12/23:13–36. The first full unit follows a section on the wrath of God that will be displayed at coming judgment ("who can endure to stand before His angels?"). The first instruction is a reflection on the fragility of humankind: "like grass he sprouts from his ground, and his goodliness flowers like a blossom . . . and there is no hope (for him). And he – his days are like a shadow over the land." The language and content of these reflections are familiar from Isaiah 40:6–8; Psalms 90:5–6; 103:15–16; and Job 14:1.

The second instruction (i 13–ii 3) is a challenge to "draw wisdom from the might of God." The "might of God" refers to what God did for Israel in the time of the exodus: "remember the marvels He did in Egypt, and His signs in [the land of Ham]." These mighty acts are cited as reasons why those being instructed should get their own lives in order: "let your heart tremble before His dread . . . why do you give up your soul to vanity?" In its address to "my people" and its appeal to God's mighty acts during the exodus generation in a context of sapiential instruction, this second instruction is reminiscent of the sapiential meditation in Psalm 78.

The third instruction (ii 3–8) is directed to "my sons" and seems to concern the two ways and the judgment. Though the text is very fragmentary, it appears that the "words of the Lord" provide the appropriate guidance for those who wish to pursue the way of wisdom and righteousness. The addressees are told to walk "in the way He laid down for Jacob, and in the path He appointed for Isaac." In the background is the connection (or even the identification) between wisdom and Israel's Torah. How and by what one walks will have consequences in the coming judgment: "to be separated from His angels, for there is no darkness nor gloom. . . ."

The first beatitude (ii 8–13) declares "happy" the one "to whom she has been given." The beatitude is a standard wisdom form (as in Psalm 1) that points to someone as being especially fortunate or "happy." This person is declared happy because of some gift from God (a divine passive). But who or what is "she?" Is it wisdom or the Torah? Since both *ḥokmâ* and *torâ* are feminine gender nouns in Hebrew, we cannot be certain which is meant. In fact, given the tendency in this work (see the third instruction) and elsewhere (see Sirach 24:23) to equate wisdom and the Torah, there is probably no need to choose between the two options here. What is more important here is the insistence on wisdom (or the Torah) as a gift from God, a revelation, not something derived solely from human reason, ingenuity, and experience.

The first beatitude in 4Q185 is remarkable on three other counts. First, it contains part of an objection put in the mouth of a wicked person: "She has not been given to me, nor. . . ." The response appeals to the sovereignty and wisdom of God ("with a good measure He measures her out") and to the display of divine justice in the coming judgment ("all His people He will redeem; and He will slay those . . . "). Second, there is a lively admonition to pursue wisdom (or the Torah): "seek her and find her and hold fast to her and get her as an inheritance." Third, there is a list of the rewards of such a pursuit: "With her is length of days and fatness of bone and joy of heart. . . ."

The second beatitude (ii 13–iii 1) declares "happy" the one who "works" or "does" it. The "it" – wisdom or Torah? – is something to be acted upon, not merely something to be contemplated or admired. Thus the sage stands in the tradition of practical wisdom. It belonged to "his fathers" – to his ancestors in Israel. The idea of wisdom as active in Israel's history (especially in the exodus) is developed in great detail in the book of Wisdom, though in ways quite different from anything we find at Qumran. The sage in the present time has inherited this wisdom and should "hold fast to her with all the power of his strength." The sage in turn will hand this wisdom on to the generations to come: "he will give her as an inheritance to his offspring."

Despite its fragmentary character, the wisdom instruction in 4Q185 makes some important contributions to our understanding of wisdom at Qumran. It illustrates the literary conventions of the wisdom instruction. It shows that a sage can appeal both to the human condition (though in biblical terms) and to God's mighty acts in the exodus in order to exhort those being addressed to choose and stay on the way of wisdom. It suggests a close relation or even an equation between wisdom and the Torah. And it presents wisdom as both a gift from God and something that humans should pursue, embrace, act upon, and hand on to the coming generations.

6

A LARGE WISDOM
INSTRUCTION
(SAPIENTIAL WORK A)

INTRODUCTION

The most extensive wisdom writing in the Qumran library is a wisdom instruction sometimes designated as Sapiential Work A. There are substantial parts of this work in 4Q416, 417, and 418. Other parts are preserved in 1Q26, 4Q415, and 4Q423 (Milik and Barthélemy 1955: 100–2; Wacholder and Abegg 1991: 54–154, 166–71; Eisenman and Wise 1992: 241–54; Harrington and Strugnell 1993: 492–94). Since there are textual overlaps among the various manuscripts, we can be sure that they belong to the same work. All the manuscripts are written in the Herodian formal hand of the late first century BCE or early first century CE. The fact that parts of six copies exist indicates the popularity and importance of the work at Qumran (García Martínez 1994: 383–93; Harrington 1994: 137–52; Schiffman 1994: 203–6; Elgvin 1993: 137–52; 1995a: 440–63; 1995b: 559–80).

This Qumran sapiential work is a wisdom instruction expressed in small units and put together without much apparent concern for logical or thematic progression. In form and content it is similar to Sirach, parts of Proverbs (especially 22:17–24:22), late Egyptian wisdom writings, Jesus' instructions in the Synoptic Gospels, and the letter of James. In the instructional setting the senior sage gives advice to a novice sage. In some places the senior sage's appeal is to pragmatism or to reward and punishment at the judgment, while in other places there are deductions from and symbolic uses of Scripture.

Some of the language in the more theological parts of the work can be found in the so-called sectarian writings from Qumran

(Community Rule, Thanksgiving Hymns, Damascus Document, etc.). But the work presupposes a secular or non-"monastic" setting. The one being instructed engages in business, has dealings with all kinds of people, and may marry a wife and have children. These facts admit of several explanations: the work could be pre-Qumranic – before the movement became sectarian and monastic; or it could be intended for Essenes who lived a life more directly integrated into Second Temple Jewish society; or it could be designed as a step in the education and formation of those who would eventually present themselves for full membership in the movement.

Fragment 1 of 4Q416 is badly damaged – so much so that there is not a single complete line of text. Nevertheless, this fragment may be very important. Before the writing starts there is an extensive margin on the right-hand side. Such a margin would seem to designate the beginning of the work. And what can be deciphered of the beginning of the work indicates that it started with a cosmic and eschatological theological framework.

The cosmic aspect of the framework is suggested by phrases such as "season by season . . . and the host of the Heavens He has established . . . and luminaries for their portents, and signs of their festivals." The eschatological aspect is indicated by the best preserved parts of the fragment: "In heaven He shall pronounce judgment upon the work of wickedness, but all His faithful children will be accepted with favor by Him . . . and every spirit of flesh will be laid utterly bare but the sons of Heaven shall rejoice in the day when it (i.e., wickedness) is judged. And all iniquity shall come to an end until the epoch of destruction will be finished."

It would appear that the wisdom instructions that follow in the main part were intended to help the one who is being instructed both to align himself with the correct order of the cosmos (as discerned from Genesis 1 and probably on the basis of a solar calendar) and to prepare for the divine judgment when the righteous will be vindicated and wickedness will be destroyed forever. If fragment 1 of 4Q416 is indeed the beginning of the great sapiential instruction, then it must have provided the theological perspective in which the sage's advice on various issues was to be interpreted. And that perspective was cosmic and eschatological.

TEXT 1: 4Q416 2 i–iv 13
(AND PARALLEL MANUSCRIPTS)

Text

i 22 For your own sake alone do not ask for your food, for He *ii 1* has let loose His merci[es . . . so as to fi]ll up all the deficiencies of His *'wt* and to give food *2* to all that lives; and there is no [. . . if] He shuts His hand, then will be gathered in the spirit of all *3* flesh. Do not [. . .] and at his shame you will cover your face, nor at his folly *4* from the prisoner. As much as a man's creditor will lend him in money, hastily pay him back and you will be on an equal footing with him. If your treasure *5* purse you have entrusted to your creditor on account of your friends, you have given away all your life for its price. Hasten and give what *6* is his, and take back your purse, and with your words do not make yourself feeble-spirited. *7* For no price exchange your holy spirit, for there is no price of equal value to it. [. . .] not turn you away [. . .] With favor seek his presence and according to his language *8* speak, and then you will find what you wish.

[. . .] and your statutes do not abandon, and with your secrets take good care *9* of yourself. If he entrusts you with his service, let there be no rest to your soul nor sleep to your eyes until you have done *10* his commands, all of them, but no more. And it is possible to act hu[mbly . . .] and do not leave anything undone for him. Money of taxes *11* [. . .] lest he say, "He has despoiled me, and fallen is [. . ." Lift up your] eyes and see how great is the enviousness *12* of humankind and twisted the heart more than all [. . .] and if with his favor you undertake his service, and the wisdom of his *'wt 13* [. . .] you counsel him, and then you will become a firstborn son for him, and he will show pity to you as a man does to his only child, *14* [. . .] you are his servant. And you, do not try to win others' confidence lest you become hated, nor [. . .] from your oppressive tax-man; *15* and be to him like a servant in all things.

And moreover do not abase your soul before one who is not equal to you, and then you will become *16* [for him . . .]. One who does not have your strength do not smite lest you make him stumble, and your own shame you increase greatly.

17 Do not sell yourself for money. It is good for you to become a servant in spirit so that for no wages you may serve your oppressors. And not for any price *18* do you sell your glory, and do not give in surety your inheritance lest it dispossess also your body.

Do not sate yourself with food *19* when there is no clothing, and do not drink wine when there is no food; do not seek after luxury when you *20* lack bread. Do not esteem yourself highly for your poverty when you are a pauper lest *21* you bring into contempt your own life.

And moreover do not dishonor the vessel of your bosom (or, your lawful vessel) . . .

iii 2 and remember that you are poor [. . .] And what you need *3* you will not find, and in your treacherousness you will [. . .].

If a deposit has been deposited with you, *4* do not reach forth your hand against it lest you (or, it) be scorched and your body be burnt in its fire. Just as you have taken it, so restore it; *5* and joy there is to you if you are exempt from any obligation arising from it.

And moreover from any man whom you have known take no property, *6* lest it increase your poverty. And if he put it to the responsibility of your head until death, deposit it but let not your spirit be taken as a pledge *7* for it. And then you will sleep with confidence, and at your death your memory will flower forever, and your posterity will inherit *8* joy.

You are poor. Do not desire something beyond your share, and do not be confused by it, lest you displace *9* your boundary. But if they cause you to dwell in splendor, walk in it, and by the mystery that is to be/come study its origins. And then you will know *10* what is allotted to it and in righteousness you will walk. For God will cause to shine His . . . upon all your ways. To Him who glorifies you give honor, *11* and praise His name always. For out of poverty He has lifted up your head, and with nobles He has seated you, and in a glorious *12* inheritance He has placed you in authority. Seek out His favor always.

You are poor. Do not say, "I am poor, and I will not *13* study knowledge." Bring your shoulder under all instruction and with all [. . .] purify your heart and with abundance of understanding *14* (purify) your thoughts. Study the mystery that is to be/come, and understand all the ways of truth, and all the roots of iniquity *15* you shall contemplate. And then you will know what is bitter for a man and what is sweet for a fellow.

Honor your father in your poverty *16* and your mother in your low estate. For as God is to man, so is his father; and as a master is to a fellow, so is his mother. For *17* they are the smelting-pot/womb that was pregnant with you. And just as He set them in authority over you and . . . according to the spirit, so serve them, and as *18* they uncovered your ear to the mystery that is to be/come, honor them for the sake of your own honor; and with reverence venerate their presence *19* for the sake of your life and the length of your days.

And if you are poor as [. . .] *20* without statute. You have taken a wife in your poverty; take her offspring in your lowly estate [. . .] *21* from the mystery that is to be/come while you keep company together. Walk together with the helpmeet of your flesh [. . .] *iv 1* his father and his mother [. . .] *2* you He has set in authority over her, [. . .] her father *3* He has not set in authority over her; from her mother He has separated her, and toward you shall be [her desire, and she will become] *4* for you one flesh. Your daughter to another He will separate, and your sons [. . .] *5* And you will be made into a unity with the wife of your bosom for she is flesh of your nakedness; *6* and the one who claims authority over her apart from you has displaced the boundary of his life.

Over her spirit *7* He has set you in authority so that she should walk in your good pleasure, and let her not make numerous vows and votive offerings; *8* turn her spirit to your good pleasure. And every oath binding on her, to vow a vow, *9* annul it according to a (mere) utterance of your mouth; and at your good pleasure restrain her from performing [. . .] by a (mere) utterance *10* of your lips. Forgive her [. . .] for your own sake. Do not let her increase [. . .] *11* your glory in your inheritance [. . .] *12* in your inheritance, lest [. . .] *13* the wife of your bosom, and shame [. . .].

Exposition

The best preserved section of Sapiential Text A is 4Q416, fragment 2. There are four connected columns of about twenty-one lines; two columns (ii and iii) are well preserved, and two (i and iv) are very fragmentary. The text consists of instructions given by a senior sage to one apparently in need of advice. Most units begin with a second person singular imperative ("pay him back . . . hasten and give . . . lift up your eyes and see") or with a negative admonition ("do not . . ."). The form and tone of the instructions are like Proverbs 22:17–24:22, which in turn are related to the Egyptian Instruction of Amenemopet and the Aramaic Words of Ahiqar. Many of the topics have general appeal, and the advice given on them would apply in various life-settings. But some of the language at least suggests a relation to what was or what became the Qumran sect.

Only a few words from the bottom left of column i can be read. The second column begins with reflections on God's care for creation and on sensitivity to the embarrassment of another. The better preserved parts of column ii give advice about paying back loans or surety bonds quickly, maintaining integrity in business and in serving others, the rewards for serving God or one's master, avoiding what is hateful and oppressive and inappropriate, selling yourself or your soul for money or possessions, balance in acquiring possessions and in boasting over poverty, and relating to one's wife ("the vessel of your bosom," see 1 Thessalonians 4:4).

The third column is punctuated with reminders about the poverty of the one who is receiving the instruction: "remember that you are poor . . . you are poor . . . you are poor . . . if you are poor" (lines 2, 8, 12, 19). Whether this is spiritual poverty or material poverty (or both) is hard to say. This poverty, however, seems to be more a reality of the human condition and a sign of human limitations than an ideal to strive for. The instructions in the third and fourth columns concern caring for and restoring what has been deposited, caution about accepting property or money from a stranger, and not desiring more than what God has allotted. Then after encouragement to study "the mystery that is to be/come," there is advice about honoring one's parents, living in harmony with one's wife and children, exercising dominion over one's wife, and the power to annul one's wife's vows and votive offerings.

The one being instructed in all of this is a young male, much as in the book of Sirach. It is assumed that the one being instructed lives

45

"in the world," since almost all the advice concerns finances, social relations, and family relations. It is not certain whether these topics were in fact the main subjects of the work as a whole, or whether they take on such importance due to the accidents of the manuscripts' preservation. At any rate, finances and social/family relationships would not be the overwhelming concerns of those Essenes who lived an isolated or "monastic" life according to what is outlined in the Community Rule or what is generally imagined to have gone on at Qumran.

The advice about money and possessions in 4Q416 2 ii and iii is fairly conventional. The one being instructed is urged to acknowledge God as the ultimate source of sustenance for all creation: "For your own sake alone do not ask for your food, for He has let loose His mercies . . . and to give food to all that lives." He is told to pay back loans as soon as possible so as to get back on an equal footing with his creditor. Likewise, he is urged to extricate himself quickly from situations in which he has guaranteed the loan of a friend (see ii 4–6).

Later he is told not to sell his soul or self for money (ii 17). Whether this refers to going into debt or selling oneself into slavery is not clear; perhaps the latter is only the extreme case of the former. There is also a call to balance and moderation in one's lifestyle: "Do not sate yourself with food when there is no clothing, and do not drink wine when there is no food; do not seek after luxury when you lack bread" (ii 18–20).

The advice about money and possessions continues in column iii. The one being instructed is frequently reminded that he is poor. He is told to avoid tampering with a deposit deposited with him "lest you (or, it = your hand) be scorched, and your body be burnt in its fire" (iii 4–5). He is told also to avoid financial dealings with strangers "lest it increase your poverty" (iii 6). The best path is moderation: "Do not desire something beyond your share." But if good fortune comes your way "walk in it" (iii 8–9). Under no condition should the one being instructed use his poverty as an excuse for not studying wisdom and becoming wise: "Do not say, 'I am poor, and I will not study knowledge'" (iii 12–13). Poverty is no excuse: "Bring your shoulder under all instruction . . . and with abundance of understanding (purify) your thoughts" (iii 13–14). The poverty spoken about here and elsewhere in the work does not seem to be a spiritual ideal (as in Franciscan poverty or in various ascetic movements). Rather, it reflects the realities of life in the world for those who (wisely) pursue higher goals and serves as a symbol for the limitations inherent in the human condition.

Interspersed with and sometimes attached to the instructions on money and possessions is advice about social relations. Much of this material is unfortunately fragmentary and obscure, and so it is often hard to be sure of what is being said. The instructor urges the one being instructed in his financial dealings (as we have seen) to guard his autonomy and independence, so as to be on an equal footing with others and not to sell his soul or exchange his "holy spirit" for money. He is to strive eagerly to please his superiors: "If he entrusts you with his service, let there be no rest to your soul nor sleep to your eyes until you have done his commands, all of them, but no more" (ii 9–10). On the other hand, he is not to assert his superiority over those who are inferior to him: "And moreover do not abase your soul before one who is not equal to you. . . . One who does not have your strength do not smite lest you make him stumble, and your own shame you increase greatly" (ii 15–16).

These conventional pieces of advice on social relations are given a fresh perspective with the ideas that God is the real source of importance and status for human beings, that God's values are not necessarily those of humans, and that God has granted (or will grant) the one being instructed a new and glorious identity: "For out of poverty He has lifted up your head, and with nobles He has seated you, and in a glorious inheritance He has placed you in authority" (iii 11–12). The precise moment or occasion for this transformation remains obscure. Is it in turning from the way of iniquity and to the way of righteousness? Is it in joining the movement in its pre-sectarian or sectarian form? Is it in the decision to embark upon the course of study and formation, part of which is this wisdom instruction? Or is it in the everyday life of the movement, which in turn prepares for and reflects the ideal situation when God's reign of righteousness will be fully established?

The section on family relationships (iii 15–iv 13) paraphrases and expands biblical texts. The first topic is parents: "Honor your father in your poverty and your mother in your low estate" (see Exodus 20:12; Deuteronomy 5:16). This duty to honor one's parents is based upon their initial role in the start of a person's life ("the smelting-pot/womb that was pregnant with you"), the social hierarchy established by God ("and just as He set them in authority over you"), their contribution to the person's religious education ("they uncovered your ear to the mystery that is to be/come"), and the benefits that fulfilling such an obligation will bring ("for the sake of your own honor . . . for the sake of your life and the length of your days").

The section on relations with one's wife takes as its main texts Genesis 2:24 ("therefore a man leaves his father and mother and clings to his wife, and they become one flesh") and 3:16 ("your desire shall be for your husband, and he shall rule over you"). The advice in iii 20–iv 6 assumes that the one being instructed will take a wife. But it warns against being distracted "from the mystery that is to be/come while you keep company together." It makes a special point of insisting that God has set the husband (and not the wife's parents!) in authority over the wife: It is "you He has set in authority over her . . . her father He has not set in authority over her; from her mother He has separated her" (iv 2–3).

A particular case of the husband's authority over his wife concerns his power to annul her vows and votive offerings. The biblical basis for the advice is provided by Numbers 30:6–15. The rationale appears to have been the fear that the wife's generosity might bankrupt the husband. And so the advice is this: "And every oath binding on her to vow a vow, annul it according to a (mere) utterance of your mouth; and at your good pleasure restrain her from performing [. . .] by a (mere) utterance of your lips" (iv 8–10).

A more restricted teaching about annuling the wife's vows appears in the Damascus Document xvi 10–12. Though not a wisdom text in itself but containing some wisdom vocabulary and themes, the Damascus Document presupposes the kind of secular life-setting relative to money and business matters that Sapiential Work A does. These links may help to locate the Qumran wisdom materials in the broader Jewish movement behind the texts.

The three main topics of 4Q416, fragment 2 – money and possessions, social relations, and family relations – are accompanied by repeated exhortations to study the *rāz nihyeh* ("the mystery that is to be/come"). The longest and best preserved exhortation runs as follows: "Study the mystery that is to be/come, and understand all the ways of truth, and all the roots of iniquity you shall contemplate. And then you will know what is bitter for a man and what is sweet for a fellow" (iii 14–15).

In the formula *rāz* (a Persian loanword found frequently in Daniel 2) means "mystery" (Brown 1968; Coppens 1990: 132–58; Rigaux 1957–58: 237–62). The second member *nihyeh* is a niphal participle of the verb "to be" (*hāyâ*). It appears to have a future sense here and elsewhere ("the mystery that is to be/come"), and its occurrences in their contexts suggest that it has both cosmic and eschatological dimensions, as well as moral or practical consequences. Here the instructor promises that study of the "mystery that is to be/come" will give one knowledge about "all the ways of truth and all the roots of iniquity."

Earlier the sage promises that study of the "mystery that is to be/come" will lead to knowledge about "what is allotted" and enable one to walk in righteousness (iii 9–10). One of the reasons why the one being instructed should honor his parents is that "they uncovered your ear to the mystery that is to be/come" (iii 18). The one being instructed is warned not to allow his wife to distract him from the "mystery that is to be/come" (iii 20–21).

What is the "mystery that is to be/come?" It seems to be a body of teaching that concerns behavior and eschatology (Harrington 1996). It is probably an extrabiblical compendium, not the Torah. It may have been something like the "Instruction on the Two Spirits" in 1QS iii 13–iv 26. Or it may have been the "Book of Meditation" (see 1QSa i 6–8) by which a prospective member of the movement was instructed (at home?) between the ages of ten and twenty. Or it may have been the "Book of Mysteries" (1Q27, 4Q299–301), which uses the term frequently in a cosmic context.

TEXT 2: 4Q417 1 i

Text

1 at every time lest he conjure (or, sate) you. And according to his spirit speak against him lest he [. . .] *2* without reproaching the noble forgive him. And he who is bound up [. . .] *3* And moreover do not confuse his spirit for in silence you have spoken [. . .] *4* and make haste to recount his rebuke, and do not overlook your own sins [. . .] *5* He will declare righteous like you, for He is a prince among prin[ces . . .] *6* will He work. For how unique is He among every creature so as not to [. . .]

7 And a man of iniquity do not count as a helper. And moreover let there be no enemy among your friends so that they do not harm you [. . .] *8* the wickedness of his deeds together with its/his punishment. And know in what way you may walk with him [. . . let . . .] *9* not be removed from your heart. And not for yourself alone shall you increase your appetite/greed in your poverty [. . .]; *10* for what is more insignificant than a poor man? And do not rejoice in your mourning lest you have trouble in your life.

Gaze upon the mystery *11* that is to be/come, and understand the birth-time of salvation, and know who is to inherit glory and trouble. Has not rejoicing been appointed for the contrite of spirit *12* and for those among them who mourn eternal joy?

Be an advocate for your own interests, and let not [your soul be . . .] *13* to every perversity of yours. Pronounce your judgments like a righteous ruler; do not [. . .] *14* and do not overlook your own sins. Be like a humble man . . . [. . .] judgment [. . .] *15* take. And then God will appear, and His anger will turn back, and He will overlook your sin. For before the wra[th of His anger] *16* none will stand. And who will be declared righteous when He gives judgment? And without forgiveness, how will there stand before Him *17* any poor man?

And you lack food in your poverty and your surpluses [. . .] *18* you leave them over, carry (him) to the haven of his desire and take your share from him and do not (take) any more [. . .] *19* And if you lack, borrow without having a pittance of money, for [your] treasury He will not empty. [But in it according to] *20* His command everything shall come into being; and that which He gives you for food eat (it), and do not (eat) any more lest [you sh]orten *21* your life.

If men's money you borrow for your poverty, do not let there be [sleep for] you *22* day and night, nor rest for your soul [. . . until] you have restored to your creditor [his money]. Do not lie *23* to him lest you bear guilt. And moreover from reproach to your creditor [. . . and do not entrust] it further to his neighbor. *24* And against your poverty he will shut his hand. Your strength [. . .] and like him borrow, and know Him who has lent it to you.

25 And if a flogging befalls you and it [hasten . . . pa]in, do not conceal from him who [flogs you] *26* lest he uncover your reproach [. . .] a ruler over him, and then *27* he will not smite him with a rod [. . . thirty-] nine *28* and no more.

And moreover, you [O understanding child . . .] . . .

Exposition

The next best preserved part of Sapiential Text A is 4Q417, fragment 1. Column i is twenty-eight lines, much of which is fairly well intact. The major topics are the standard wisdom concerns of social relations and finances. It too contains an appeal to study the "mystery that is to be/come." Once more the senior sage gives advice to the one being instructed with imperatives ("forgive") and prohibitions ("do not confuse . . . do not overlook").

The first legible instruction (1 i 2–6) appears to concern sensitivity in the correction of others: "without reproaching the noble forgive him . . . for in silence you have spoken . . . and make haste to recount his rebuke." The rationale for this sensitivity seems to be first of all the recognition of one's own sinfulness: "do not overlook your own sins." Even more basic, however, is one's own experience of having been forgiven by God: (others) [= sinners] God "will declare righteous like you . . . (with all forgiveness) will He work." The idea of willingness to forgive others on the basis of having been forgiven by God is, of course, prominent in the New Testament (see Matthew 6:12, 14–15).

The second instruction (i 7–9) warns against associating with evil persons: "And a man of iniquity do not count as a helper. And moreover let there be no enemy among your friends." The third instruction (i 9–10) consists of two parts, and it is hard to know how they are related. The first part ("And not for yourself alone shall you increase your appetite/greed in your poverty [. . .]; for what is more insignificant than a poor man?") cautions against greed or gluttony. The second part ("do not rejoice in your mourning lest you have trouble in your life") is even more mysterious – perhaps a warning against inappropriate behavior in response to the misfortunes of others.

The fourth instruction (i 10–12) is very important for understanding the "mystery that is to be/come" mainly because of the parallel expressions: "Gaze upon the mystery that is to be/come, and understand the birth-time of salvation, and know who is to inherit glory and trouble." The eschatological dimension of the "mystery that is to be/come" is supported by synonyms "the birth-time of salvation" and "who is to inherit glory and trouble." The eschatological orientation is further confirmed by the accompanying question: "Has not rejoicing been appointed for the contrite of spirit and for those among them who mourn eternal joy?" The language and concepts are reminiscent of the Matthean beatitudes (see Matthew 5:3–12).

The fifth instruction (i 12–17) gives advice about integrity ("be an advocate for your own interests . . . pronounce your judgments like a righteous ruler . . . be like a humble man") along with a picture of God's judgment: "And then God will appear, and His anger will turn back, and He will overlook your sin. For before the wrath of His anger none will stand. And who will be declared righteous when He gives judgment? And without forgiveness how will there stand before Him any poor man?" There seems to be a connection once more between one's willingness to look at one's own sins ("and do not overlook your own sins") and God's willingness to overlook one's sins at the judgment ("and He will overlook your sin").

The rest of the column (or what can be read of it) concerns financial matters. The first instructions concern scarcity and surplus (i 17–18), willingness to borrow (i 19), and confidence that God will supply what is necessary: "according to His command everything shall come into being; and that which He gives you for food eat it" (i 20). Then after a clear instruction to pay back loans quickly ("do not let there be sleep for you day or night, nor rest for your soul") and to be honest with one's creditor (i 21–22), there are fragmentary and thus obscure teachings about financial dealings and the punishments that one may have to endure in them. The punishment here may be quite specific – flogging. If so, there may be a reference to thirty-nine strokes as in 2 Corinthians 11:24: "and then he will not smite him with a rod [. . . thirty-]nine and no more" (i 27–28).

TEXT 3: 4Q417 2 i/4Q418 43

Text

1 [. . .] You, O understanding one [. . .] *2* [. . .] gaze, and on the wondrous mysteries of the God of the Awesome Ones. You will ponder the beginning [. . .] *3* [. . .] and gaze [. . .] of old to what is, and what is to be *4* in what [. . .] to what is *5* and to what is to be in [. . .] in all [. . . every] act and act [. . .].

6 By day and by night meditate on the mystery that is to be/come, and study it always. And then you will know truth and iniquity; wisdom *7* and foolishness you will [. . .] act [. . .]

in all their ways together with their punishment(s) in all ages everlasting and the eternal *8* punishment. Then you will discern between good and evil according to their works. For the God of knowledge is the foundation of truth, and by the mystery that is to be/come *9* He has laid out its foundation, and its deeds He has prepared with [. . .] wisdom, and with all cunning He has fashioned it. And the domain of its deeds *10* [. . .] He expounded for their understanding every deed so that he could walk *11* in the inclination of his understanding. And He expounded for hu[mankind . . .], and in purity of understanding were made known the secrets *12* of his plan together with how he should walk perfect[ly in all his wo]rks. These things investigate always, and gain understanding [about a]ll *13* their outcomes. And then you will know the glory of His might together with His marvelous mysteries and His mighty acts.

And you, *14* O understanding one, study (or, inherit) your reward, remembering the requital for it comes. Engraved is the ordinance, and ordained is all the punishment. *15* For engraved is that which is ordained by God against all the iniquities of the children of Seth. And written in His presence is a book of memorial *16* of those who keep His word. And that is the vision of meditating (or, Hagu) on a book of memorial. And He gave it as an inheritance to humankind (or, Enosh) together with a spiritual people.

For *17* according to the pattern of the Holy Ones is his fashioning. But no more has meditation been given to fleshly spirit, for it knew not the difference between *18* good and evil according to the judgment of its spirit.

And you, O understanding child, gaze on the mystery that is to be/come and know *19* the paths of everything that lives and the manner of his walking that is appointed over his deeds [. . .] *20* [. . .] between great and small, and in your council [. . .] *21* [. . .] in the mystery that is to be/come [. . .] *22* [. . .] every vision [. . .] know, and in all [. . .] *23* and act with strength always. Do not weary yourself by evildoing [. . .] *24* with it he will not be guiltless. According to his inheritance in [. . .] *25* O sage child, show understanding about your mysteries and about the [. . .] *26* founded on you [. . .] together with the reward [. . .] *27* Do not go astray after your heart and after your eyes [. . .].

Exposition

Two partial copies of this text survive – one in 4Q417 2 i, and the other in 4Q418 43. The two can be joined to produce a fairly full (if none the less often obscure) passage. The text is an exhortation to the one being instructed ("You, O understanding one," lines 1, 13–14, 18) to apply himself to the "mystery that is to be/come." Study of that mystery will bring knowledge of the world and creation, of correct behavior in the present, and of the rewards and punishments accompanying the eschatological visitation.

The exhortation preserved in 4Q417 2 i and 4Q418 43 may have come from an early part of the work, perhaps shortly after the cosmological/eschatological framework set forth in 4Q416 1 and before the more mundane sapiential instructions in 4Q416 2 i–iv and 4Q417 1 i. There is, however, no certainty on this matter since such exhortations could have punctuated the work (as in Sirach) so as to win more perfect attention.

The text begins with a familiar address: "You, O understanding one." What can be retrieved from the very fragmentary and obscure lines 1–5 is the directive to gaze on "the wondrous mysteries of the God of the Awesome Ones (= angels?)," which seems to be synonymous with the "mystery that is to be/come." Such study will be repaid with knowledge of the past (". . . of old"), the present ("what is"), and the future ("what is to be").

The first large block of fairly legible material (4Q417 2 i 6–13) sheds light on the elusive "mystery that is to be/come." One who meditates on it "by day and by night" is promised knowledge of "truth and iniquity; wisdom and foolishness" as well as "their punishment(s) in all ages everlasting and the eternal punishment." Thus the "mystery" includes ethical knowledge as well as indications of the historical and eschatological consequences of human actions.

The next section (4Q417 2 i 8–10) relates this moral knowledge ("you will discern between good and evil") to God's own plan for creation and its future: "For the God of knowledge is the foundation of truth, and by the mystery that is to be/come He has laid out its (= truth's) foundation, and its deeds He has prepared with . . . wisdom. . . ." The epithet "God of knowledge," which appears in 1 Samuel 2:3, occurs at the beginning of the "Instruction on the Two Spirits" in 1QS iii 13–iv 26. At Qumran it refers to the sovereign God who has ultimate authority and His letting history unfold according to His providence until the final "visitation."

What follows in 4Q417 2 i 10–12 is hard to understand. But the point seems to be that God (?) has set forth or expounded for humans what they need to know in order to walk perfectly before God. The section ends in lines 12–13 with another exhortation to meditate on and absorb these matters: "These things investigate always, and gain understanding about all their outcomes. And then you will know the glory of His might together with His marvelous mysteries and His mighty acts." Thus the object of meditation ("the mystery that is to be/come") has several aspects: creation or the cosmos, moral behavior or ethics, God or theology, and eschatology.

The second large block of legible material (4Q417 2 i 13–18) concerns divine judgment on human acts. It begins with the address found elsewhere in the column (lines 1 and 18): "And you, O understanding (or, discerning) one." The addressee is told to "study (or, inherit) your reward, remembering the requital, for it comes." Then using the motif of the heavenly tablets or books (see also Jubilees 30:20–22; 1 Enoch 47:3; 108:3) and drawing on the language of Exodus 32:16, the instructor warns: "Engraved is the ordinance, and ordained is all the punishment. For engraved is that which is ordained by God against all the iniquities of the children of Seth." This heavenly tablet or book apparently contains a list of evil deeds and the punishments that can be expected to follow on them as consequences (Lange 1995a: 69–79).

The reference to the "children of Seth" is very peculiar. It may allude to Balaam's prophecy that Israel "will crush the borderlands of Moab and the territory of all the Shethites" (Numbers 24:17). If so, then the "children of Seth" is a biblical allusion to the enemies of God (and Israel). If the reference is to Genesis 4:25 ("Adam knew his wife again, and she bore a son and named him Seth"), then the allusion is to the patriarch Seth. But then why the focus on the "iniquities" of the children of Seth? A reference to Numbers 24:17 seems more likely (see also 1QM xi 6; CD vii 21; and 4Q Testimonia). Its use here may reflect the integration of prophetic/eschatological material into the wisdom tradition – a move also suggested by the description of David as both sage and prophet in the prose summary of David's compositions in the Cave 11 Psalms Scroll.

The text goes on to mention a second heavenly tablet or book containing the names of the righteous: "And written in His presence is a book of memorial of those who keep His word." The language is taken from Malachi 3:16: "a book of remembrance was written before Him of those who revered the Lord and thought on

His name." The biblical context is eschatological and includes the figure of Elijah, who is a figure in Qumran eschatology. Meditating on this book of memorial (is it part of the "mystery that is to be/come?") has been granted to humankind (or, Enosh [the son of Seth], see Genesis 4:26?) – or at least to those who constitute "a spiritual people." It has not been granted to "fleshly spirit, for it knew not the difference between good and evil." Behind these images of the heavenly books showing evil deeds and their consequences as well as the names of those who keep God's word are the theological problems of predestination, election, and human freedom that surface in the sectarian Qumran documents (especially in the Community Rule [see iii 13–iv 26] and Hodayot) and that emerge in various forms in later Jewish and Christian theology.

The next unit (4Q417 2 i 18ff.) begins with a form of the customary address ("And you, O understanding child") and urges meditation on the "mystery that is to be/come," which in turn will yield knowledge of "the paths of everything that lives." The rest of the column, which is quite fragmentary, seems to be an exhortation to act upon the knowledge that one gains by applying oneself to the "mystery that is to be/come": "Do not weary yourself by evildoing . . . Do not go astray after your heart and after your eyes."

The second column of 4Q417 2 continues in the same vein (though very little of it is preserved). In language like that of the Community Rule, it offers instructions to "walk perfectly" (ii 5) and to bless God's name and to praise God (ii 6, 9), even in times of suffering ("despite every stroke," ii 9). There are also warnings about punishment for evil deeds: "He will punish all your ways" (ii 11). What is especially interesting here is the admonition: "Let not the thought of an evil inclination mislead you . . ." (ii 12). The "evil inclination" is the *yēṣer rāʿ* that can prompt a person to sin. In 1QS iv 15–16 the cosmic struggle between Light and Darkness also includes the individual: "and all the reward of their deeds shall be forever according to whether each one's portion in their divisions is great or small." Later Jewish texts paired the evil inclination with the good inclination, and regarded the human person as subject to a battle within the self. Christian theology developed from this idea the notion of concupiscence – the innate (due to original sin) human tendency toward sin. Such language at the end of column 1 and in column 2 could have provided the introductory framework to the more conventional sapiential instructions that appear in 4Q416 2 i–iv and 4Q417 1 i.

OTHER FRAGMENTS

Sapiential Work A seems to have been a long text. Nevertheless, even though many parts of it survive, most of it exists only in very fragmentary form. Given the modest scope of this introduction to wisdom at Qumran, here we can only point to a few highlights in the remaining fragments.

4Q415 2 ii 1–9 appears to give advice to a woman – the wife of the one being instructed in most of the work. The format is the instruction cast in singular imperatives and singular prohibitions. But unlike most of the work, this part uses the feminine verbal forms of the imperatives and prohibitions. Since column i of 4Q415 2 uses the masculine forms, this section represents a change of addressee and a change of subject.

The advice to the woman is quite conventional and in keeping with the patriarchal assumptions of the better preserved parts of the work. She is told to honor her father-in-law (?) as her own father, to cling to her husband's bosom, not to neglect her "holy covenant" (the marriage bond), and be a "subject of praise on the mouth of all men." Although the advice is conventional, the fact that a woman is directly addressed in a wisdom instruction is highly unusual in Jewish wisdom literature.

Another emphasis that is unusual in Jewish wisdom literature (but well documented in other Qumran texts) is the correlation between the angels in heaven and the righteous on earth: "angels of holiness serve Him in heaven; but the earth He has given over to the sons of truth, and they will follow after all the roots of understanding" (4Q418 55 8–9). Nevertheless, to exhort the righteous not to grow weary in seeking wisdom, the instructor uses the example of the "sons of heaven, whose lot is eternal life" (4Q418 69 12–13). Whether the point of the comparison is the angels' untiring enjoyment of wisdom or their glorious existence with God as a goal for the righteous to pursue, is not entirely clear. The latter point is developed at some length in 4Q418 81 in which the one being instructed is assured of a place with God's holy ones in the heavenly court: "among all the godly ones He has cast your lot, and has magnified your glory greatly, and has appointed you as a first-born . . . saying 'I will bless you'" (4–5). The description "first-born" most likely is a synonym for one who is especially loved by God. This (hoped for) assimilation of the "holy ones" on earth to the holy ones in heaven becomes a major theme in some of the more explicitly sectarian texts (as in the Songs of the Sabbath Sacrifice). And there is some indication that the sect's rules and regulations were intended to attune or put in line its members with what was reckoned to be taking place in the heavenly court (see 1QSa ii, War Scroll, etc.).

The work also seems to have used the threat of eschatological sanctions as a motive for wise and appropriate behavior in the present. 4Q418 69 addresses in turn "you foolish ones" (4–9) and "the chosen by truth" (10–15). What is unusual is the second person plural mode of address in a work where the singular mode predominates. There may have been a change in the rhetorical situation, or perhaps the incorporation of pre-existing material into the work at this point. The foolish ones are warned that "to the everlasting pit shall your return be . . . its dark places shall cry out . . . those who investigate the truth shall be roused up for your judgment" (6–7). The final destiny of the foolish is annihilation: "Then will all the foolish ones in mind be destroyed, and the children of iniquity shall not be found anymore, and all those who hold fast to wickedness shall wither away" (8). In 4Q418 126 ii the righteous are promised that "upon the power of God and the greatness of His glory together with His goodness and His great mercy shall they meditate, and upon His faithfulness shall they reflect always. Continually shall they praise His name" (9–11). Again, this kind of angelic existence is what the Qumran sect took as their ideal mode of existence on earth. Heaven is the extension of life in the community – only without time limit and the distractions and discouragements of everyday life.

Several sections of the work use agricultural imagery (for example 4Q418 103; 4Q423 2, 5). Is this advice to farmers? Or is the talk about agriculture metaphorical, that is a way of teaching about the moral life and the final judgment (or, "harvest")? There are references to plowmen, baskets, barns, and seasons (4Q418 103 2–5). There are also references to fruits of produce, trees pleasant and delightful to contemplate, and a garden (4Q423 2 1–3) that evoke Genesis 2–3. There are instructions about observing "the festivals of the summer" and gathering in your harvest in its time and about contemplating "all your harvest" (4Q423 5 6–7). But the metaphorical application (if there is one) remains elusive. Perhaps a large section assumed that the one being instructed would be a farmer of some sort (but compare Sirach 38:25–26).

Another unusual feature in this work is the incorporation of biblical legal material in wisdom instruction. We have already looked at the use of Numbers 30:6–15 in the instruction about the husband's power to annul the vows and votive offerings of his wife (4Q416 2 iv). So also in one of the agricultural texts (4Q418 103) the best preserved part invokes the biblical law of "mixed things" from Leviticus 19:19 and Deuteronomy 22:9–11: "Moreover with your own merchandise do not mix that which is your neighbor's, lest it be mixed species like a mule and you become as one who wears mixed cloth, of wool and flax . . ." (6–7). The biblical ruling is adapted to the format of the wisdom instruction and used as a consideration (without an appeal to the authority of the Torah) in sapiential advice. The problem of the referent – agriculture or some aspect of the moral life – remains. In 4QMMT B:75–82 the law of "mixed things" is invoked in the course of a halakhic argument about illegal marriages between members of priestly and non-priestly families.

7

OTHER QUMRAN WISDOM INSTRUCTIONS

INTRODUCTION

None of the other Qumran wisdom texts is nearly so extensive as Sapiential Work A. Nevertheless, some are quite substantial and make important contributions to our picture of wisdom at Qumran. 4Q424 describes persons to be avoided (if you want something done) and persons to be cultivated as friends (for their intellectual and moral character). 4Q420–421 describes the characteristics of a wise and righteous person. 4Q413 begins or introduces a hymn about acquiring wisdom. Likewise, 4Q298 begins or introduces the speech of the *maśkil* to the "sons of dawn." All these works are fragments of wisdom instructions in which the speaker addresses an individual or a group and explains to them how to act wisely in human society or in an even more cosmic framework.

The most extensive of the other Qumran wisdom texts is 4Q525 – also known as 4Q Beatitudes because it features a series of at least five beatitudes. In fact, there is far more to this text than beatitudes (though much of that is very fragmentary). The Book of Mysteries represented by 1Q27 and 4Q299, 300, and perhaps 301 sheds more light on the "mystery that is to be/come" and provides an eschatological scenario, thus confirming the link between wisdom and eschatology that is so characteristic of wisdom at Qumran.

TEXT 1: 4Q424

Text

Fragment 1: *4* [. . .] With a dissembler do not take up a lawsuit, and with a shaky person do not *5* go into a furnace, for like lead so he will be melted and not stand before fire.

6 In the hand of a fool do not entrust a secret (?), for he will not conceal your business; and do not send word *7* to a dull person, for he will not smooth out your ways.

A man who is always complaining – do not expect from him *8* to receive wealth for your needs.

A man devious in speech – do not trust him to pronounce *9* judgment in your favor; he will surely be devious in speech; after truth he will not run [but will harm you] *10* by the fruit of his lips.

A man with an evil eye (i.e., greedy, jealous, envious) – do not appoint him over [your wealth, for he will not] *11* mete out your residue to your satisfaction [. . .] *12* and in the time of accounting he will be found a hypocrite.

One who is short-tempered – do not appoint him [to judge] *13* the simple, for he will surely devour them.

Fragment 3: *1* [. . .] A man who judges before he investigates and believes before [he tests] *2* – do not appoint him over the seekers of knowledge, for he will not understand their judgment – so as to declare just the righteous and to declare guilty the wicked. *3* He too will be an object of contempt.

A man whose eyes are smeared over – do not send to discern (or, spy out) for the upright, for [he will lead them astray].

[A man] *4* hard of hearing – do not send to investigate a case, for a dispute among men he will not smooth out. Like one who winnows in a [weak] wind *5* that cannot purify, so is one who speaks to an ear that does not hear, and pronounces their vow to one slumbering in a spirit of [. . .]

6 A man with an unreceptive mind (lit., fat of heart) – do not send to dig out plots, for the wisdom of his heart is hidden, and he has no control over [. . .], *7* and the wisdom of his hands he will not find.

A man of intelligence will accept instruction.

A man who knows will find wisdom.

8 An upright man will delight in justice.

A man of truth will rejoice in a proverb.

A man of substance will be zealous for [. . . and he] *9* will be an opponent to all those who move a boundary.

A man of generosity will give charity to the poor [. . .] *10* to all those lacking wealth, sons of righteousness [. . .]

Exposition

Two relatively well preserved fragments (1 and 3) of 4Q424 (Wacholder and Abegg 1991: 174–76; Eisenman and Wise 1992: 166–68; García Martínez 1994: 393–94; Vermes 1995: 278–79) take up a common topic in sapiential works – persons to be cautious about or to avoid, and persons to cultivate and to befriend. The form is admonition ("do not . . .") and instruction, not the proverb strictly defined (despite the putative title given to the work, 4QProverbs). All of what can be read in fragment 1 and most of what can be read in fragment 3 concern persons who are best avoided, especially for carrying out certain legal and commercial tasks.

The instructor giving the advice is, as usual, well experienced in human affairs. The one being instructed is (or will one day be) a "man of affairs" – someone who engages in lawsuits, commerce, and the search for wisdom. He is (or is to be) very much a "man of the world," not a monk. In fragment 1 the one being instructed is warned against taking up a lawsuit with a liar and getting involved in a trial (legal or otherwise) with a "shaky" person (424 1 4–5), against relying on fools (or lazy people) and dullards to handle his affairs (6–7), against expecting financial help from a habitual complainer (7–8), against hoping to find justice from someone who is devious in speech (8–10), against giving a greedy steward control over one's money and property (10–12), and against letting a short-tempered man judge the "simple" (12–13). In every case the assumption is that the one being instructed has (or will have) property and power in the secular sphere.

The list of persons to be avoided in fragment 3 admits of a more spiritual or moral interpretation. Again the assumption is that the one being instructed has the authority and power to send others out on some kind of mission. But the nature of the missions can here be construed as pertaining to moral or intellectual matters, rather than legal and commercial affairs. Thus the one being instructed is warned against appointing someone who judges before investigating over "the seekers of knowledge" (424 3 1–3), against sending someone with blurred (moral or intellectual?) vision to discern on behalf of the upright (3), against sending someone who is hard of hearing (morally or intellectually obtuse?) to investigate (4–5), and against sending someone who is "fat of heart" (one with an unreceptive mind, see Isaiah 6:10) to search out "plots" (6–7). The language of the second list (4Q424 3) is more metaphorical and thus more susceptible to moral or intellectual interpretations than is the first list (4Q424 1). But the language remains quite generic and elusive.

The second part of fragment 3 (lines 7–10) begins with a list of persons to be cultivated and befriended. They are persons outstanding for their intellectual and moral characteristics: intelligent, knowledgeable, upright, truthful, substantial, and generous. In each case those who already have these characteristics will get more (as in Mark 4:25). On the contrary, those who are foolish and wicked can never be trusted to make any good contribution.

The division of humankind into the wise/righteous and foolish/wicked is typical of Jewish wisdom literature. The logic is the experiential logic of secular wisdom writings. There is no hint of eschatology and divine judgment in these fragments. There may have been a reference to the Torah in 4Q424 3 8–9 in the gap that is paralleled antithetically by "all those who move a boundary." And there may have been sectarian language where fragment 3 breaks off ("sons of righteousness"). But we cannot be sure. In what can be read there is nothing Qumranian or sectarian or eschatological or even associated directly with the Torah. 4Q424 may contain the remnants of a secular sapiential work, or represent a secular section within a larger Jewish sapiential work (as in Sirach).

TEXT 2: 4QWAYS OF RIGHTEOUSNESS
(4Q420 1 ii 1–5 = 4Q421 1 ii 13–15)

Text

the prudent man [. . .] to walk in God's ways, to act righteously [. . .] *1* He will not answer before he hears, *2* and he will not speak before he understands, and with patience *3* he will give a reply. He will seek truth (and) justice, and in searching out righteousness *4* he will find its outcomes. [. . .] and a humble and contrite man, his knowledge will not turn back *5* until [. . .] a faithful man will not turn from the ways of righteousness [. . .]

Exposition

The fragments designated 4Q420 and 421 (Wacholder and Abegg 1991: 159–65) come from a wisdom composition. Though some of its vocabulary can be read in a sectarian way (see 4Q421 1 i 3–4 "order," "lot"), the most extensive piece constituted by an overlap between 4Q420 1 ii 1–5 and 4Q421 1 ii 13–15 is similar in content to the description of righteous persons in 4Q424 3 7–10. The righteous person is prudent, humble and contrite, and faithful. He walks in God's ways, is circumspect in dealing with other people, seeks out truth and justice, and never turns from the ways of righteousness. The vocabulary of the text reflects the association between wisdom and righteousness that is typical of Jewish (and Qumran) wisdom literature (as in 4Q424). Of course, at Qumran or in the movement that led to the Qumran community these typical Jewish wisdom terms could have been related to the "mystery that is to be/come" and viewed as particularly appropriate to members of the movement.

TEXT 3: HYMN OF KNOWLEDGE (4Q413)

Text

1 A psalm, a so[ng. Knowledge] and wisdom I will teach you, and get understanding in the ways of humankind and in the deeds *2* of the children of humanity. For each person God has made great for him an inheritance in the knowledge of His truth and according to his loathing *3* all evil. Whoever [hardens] his ears from hearing and his eye from seeing shall not live. And now *4* [His] . . . mercy with the people of old, and consider the years of past generations as God revealed. . . .

Exposition

The fragment (Wacholder and Abegg 1991: 43; García Martínez 1994: 383–84) is the beginning of, or perhaps the introduction to, a hymn about acquiring knowledge or wisdom (perhaps about the "mystery that is to be/come"). The first word or two ("a psalm, a song," see Psalms 66, 67) may designate it as a hymn, though in form what survives has more in common with the wisdom instructions or admonitions we have already seen. The instructor speaking in the first person singular addresses listeners in the second person plural. The instructor promises knowledge about God's plans for humankind, God's will regarding their actions, and the rewards and punishments that God will mete out. Using the language of Isaiah 6:10, he warns against hardening one's ears and eye. Using the language of Deuteronomy 32:7, he invites the listeners to remember the days of old.

On the other hand, the language ("rewards ... inheritance ... knowledge of His truth ... as God revealed") fits in with the more sectarian compositions in the Qumran corpus. Thus this little passage, hardly significant in itself, illustrates a basic methodological problem encountered in studying the Qumran wisdom texts: the combination of biblical, distinctively sectarian, and nonsectarian sapiential language in four lines of text.

TEXT 4: 4Q298 1

Text

1–2 i 1 [Wo]rd of a *maśkil* that he spoke to all the sons of dawn: "List[en to me, all] you men of heart. *2* And you who [pur]sue righteousness, understand my words. And you who seek truth, h[ea]r my words in all *3* that issues from my lips. And those who know have pursued these things and have turn[ed to the way] of life. O m[en *4* of his] good will and eternal [peace without] limit . . .

3–4 ii 3 . . . And now *4* list[en, you wise ones]; and you who know, hear. And men *5* of understanding, incr[ease learn]ing; and you who pursue justice add modesty; *6* you who [know the way], add courage; and you men *7* of truth, pur[sue righteousness]; and you lovers of lovingkindness, add *8* humility [. . .] appointed time which *9* is interpreted [. . .] you may understand the end *10* of the ages, and upon the former things you may look to know. . . .

Exposition

Much of 4Q298 (Eisenman and Wise 1992: 160–65; Pfann 1994: 203–35; Kister 1994: 237–49) is written in a cryptic or esoteric script. The *maśkil* is the spiritual guide of the community (as in the Community Rule), not an ordinary sage (Kosmala 1973: 235–41). Likewise, the "sons of dawn" is probably a technical term used to describe novices or aspirants to the community on their way to becoming full members ("sons of light"). The cryptic script may have been due to the need for the *maśkil* to meet the "sons of dawn" outside the confines of the community (the "camps" of the Damascus Document, or Qumran?) and thus to ensure that the esoteric wisdom of the group be concealed from outsiders.

The best preserved parts of the text translated above use first person singular language with regard to the instructor and second person plural forms for those being instructed (as in 4Q413 and 4Q525). These parts are somewhat formulaic calls to pay attention in the hortatory style. The first text (4Q298 1–2 i) consists of a title or heading, a call to listen, and what seems to be an appeal to the experience of those who have have found the "way of life" in the community's wisdom.

The second text (4Q298 3–4 ii) is a challenge to the wise and knowing to work at the pursuit of virtue. It is remarkable for its use of wisdom terms ("wise ones . . . you who know . . . men of understanding . . . learning . . . the way . . . truth") coupled with the prophetic-legal terminology ("justice . . . righteousness . . . lovingkindness"), a combination that is quite common in Qumran texts. The promise of understanding the "end of the ages" and "the former things" fits well the language and conceptuality of Sapiential Work A and the Book of Mysteries. What can be read of the rest of the work indicates an interest in cosmic matters ("in all the world . . . its roots . . . in the abyss below . . . boundaries") – as in other wisdom texts from Qumran.

TEXT 5: 4QBEATITUDES (4Q525)

Text

2 ii [Happy is the one who speaks truth] *1* with a pure heart and does not slander with his tongue.

Happy are they who cling to her statutes and do not cling *2* to the ways of iniquity.

Happy are they who rejoice in her and do not babble in the ways of iniquity.

Happy are they who seek her with pure hands and do not search for her *3* with a deceitful heart.

Happy is the man (who) has attained wisdom, and walks by *4* the Law of the Most High, and fixes his heart on her ways, and gives heed to her admonitions, and in her chastisements delights always, *5* and does not forsake her in the stress of his troubles; (who) in time of distress does not abandon her, and does not forget her [in days] of fear, *6* and in the affliction of his soul does not reject her. For on her he always meditates, and in his anguish he reflects [on the Law and in all] *7* his life on her [he meditates . . .] before his eyes not to walk in the ways of [iniquity] . . . *9* [. . .] and with kings she will make him sit . . . *12* and now sons, he[ar my voice, and do] not turn [from the words of my mouth . . .].

4 8 [Do not] abandon [your inheritance to the strang]er and your lot to the children of the foreigner, for the wise [. . . *9* . . .] they instruct with [. . . . Those who fear] God will keep her ways and will walk in all *10* her statutes, and her reproaches they will not reject. Those who understand will acquire [words of understanding . . . *11* . . .]; they will walk in integrity; they will keep away from iniquity, and her reproaches they will not reject [. . . *12* . . .] they will hear. The prudent dig her ways, and in her depths [. . . *13* . . .] they watch. Those who love God humble themselves for her [. . .].

14 ii [. . .] *12* your soul; He will free you from all evil, and fear will not enter you [. . .] *13* your inheritance; He will fill your days with good, with much peace [. . .] *14* you will inherit honor, and when you are taken to eternal rest they will inherit [. . .] *15* and in your teaching they will walk; all who know you will [. . .] *16* together they will mourn, and in your ways they will remember you, and you will [. . .].

18 And now understand, listen to me, and pay attention [. . .] *19* bring forth knowledge deep within you [. . .] *20* With righteous humility express [your] words [. . . do not] *21* respond with the words of your neighbor lest [. . .] *22* and as you hear answer according to it [. . . do not] *23* utter a complaint before you hear their words [. . .] *24* very much. First hear their word and then respond [. . . with] *25* patience bring them forth; and answer straightforwardly in the midst of princes [. . .] *26* and with your lips. And be very careful of a slip of the tongue [. . .] *27* lest you be conquered by your lip[s and be] trapped together by your tong[ue].

Exposition

The name given to 4Q525 – 4QBeatitudes – reflects only the best preserved part of a much longer wisdom text (Wacholder and Abegg 1991: 185–203; Eisenman and Wise 1992: 168–77; García

Martínez 1994: 395–98; Vermes 1995: 286–87). It is a sapiential instruction in which the speaker uses the first person singular ("listen to me") to address a second person plural audience ("sons"). Its most prominent feature is the series of five beatitudes in fragment 2, column ii. But it is also important for its reflections on the precious character of wisdom (which is identified with the Torah), on the rewards of wisdom and the punishments of folly, and on the need for caution in speech.

In the Hebrew Scriptures a beatitude declares someone "happy" or "fortunate." It is to be distinguished from a benediction ("blessed are you") whose object usually is God. These literary forms have become mixed up in English because translators have traditionally used "blessed" for both. In fact, the proper translation of *'ăsrê* (Hebrew)/*makarios* (Greek)/*beatus* (Latin) is "happy" whereas the proper translation of *barûk* (Hebrew)/*eulogētos* (Greek)/*benedictus* (Latin) is "blessed."

The five beatitudes (actually macarisms) most fully preserved in 4Q525 2 ii form a series – a phenomenon best attested previously in Matthew 5:3–12 and Luke 6:20–23 (see also 2 Enoch 9:1; 42:6–14; 52:1–14; Brooke 1989: 35–41; Fitzmyer 1992a: 509–15; Puech 1991: 80–106; Viviano 1993: 71–84). Unlike the New Testament macarisms which are highly eschatological ("Happy are you poor, for yours is the kingdom of God"), the macarisms in 4Q525 are sapiential (which is the usual case in the Hebrew Bible and Sirach). Indeed, the 4Q525 macarisms declare happy or fortunate those who seek and find wisdom (which is identified as the Torah).

The first four extant macarisms are short, each consisting of a positive and a negative statement. The first macarism is singular in form and echoes Psalm 15:2–3: "[Happy is the one who speaks truth] with a pure heart and does not slander with his tongue." The next three macarisms are plural in form and focus directly on wisdom and the Torah. The second macarism evokes the "two ways" imagery with respect to wisdom/Torah and iniquity: "Happy are they who cling to her statutes and do not cling to the ways of iniquity." The third macarism makes the same basic point: "Happy are they who rejoice in her and do not babble in the ways of iniquity." The fourth macarism moves backward from the possession of wisdom to the search for wisdom: "Happy are they who seek her with pure hands and do not search for her with a deceitful heart." The link between wisdom and the Torah is so close that it is hard to know whether the feminine suffixes refer to one or the other (or both!).

The fifth macarism is singular in form and breaks the positive/ negative pattern of the other four. Indeed, it is a lengthy description of one "who has attained wisdom and walks by the Law of the Most High." Note the parallelism between "wisdom" and the "Law of the Most High," and the typically biblical emphasis on wisdom as something to be practiced. Such a one "fixes his heart on her ways, and gives heed to her admonitions, and in her chastisements delights always, and does not forsake her in the stress of his troubles; (who) in time of distress does not abandon her, and does not forget her [in days] of fear, and in the affliction of his soul does not reject her. For on her he always meditates and in his anguish he reflects [on the Law] . . . ." The truly wise person learns wisdom from the Torah, which in turn sustains him in times of suffering.

The theme of the precious character of wisdom is continued in column iii. There it is said that wisdom cannot be obtained with gold or precious stones. The beauty of her face surpasses the splendor of the most beautiful woman.

The link between wisdom and the Torah is carried on in fragment 4. In language reminiscent of the wisdom psalms (especially Psalm 1), the text describes those who fear God and love God as keeping "her ways" and walking "in all her statutes." Again the feminine singular suffixes could refer to Wisdom personified or to the Torah, and indeed are probably intended to refer to both.

In fragment 14 the addressee changes from plural ("sons") to singular ("you"). In the relatively well preserved lines 12–16 the instructor recounts to the singular addressee the benefits of pursuing wisdom: it brings freedom from evil and from fear in one's lifetime ("He will free you from all evil, and fear will not enter you"); it brings the blessings of a happy life ("good . . . much peace . . . honor"). Moreover, at death the sage has the satisfaction of knowing that his teachings will be carried on by his disciples ("and in your teaching they will walk . . . in your ways they will remember you"). The shift in person from plural to singular along with the fairly specific character of the rewards that are promised (as befit a sage/teacher) suggest that this part of the work was (like much of 1Q26; 4Q415–418, 423) an instruction for prospective sages.

The second part of fragment 14 provides specific instruction on what was a favorite topic of the ancient sages – prudence in speaking. A sage was expected to be a public person, one who lived by his wits and his speech (see Sirach 39:1–11). The advice in lines 18–27 is fairly conventional: speak humbly and honestly; listen before you respond; and be very cautious about speaking among powerful people (who have the power to harm you).

The smaller and more fragmentary parts of 4Q525 appear to deal with the rewards of pursuing wisdom and the punishments of pursuing folly. The rewards of pursuing wisdom are predictable in a wisdom instruction: "it will go well with you . . . much peace . . . glory." The punishments for pursuing folly are more graphic: "darkness . . . serpents . . . fire . . . eternal curses and vipers' venom . . . the demons of death . . . flames of sulphur" (frag. 15).

TEXT 6: BOOK OF MYSTERIES

Text

(1Q27 1 i 1–12 + 4Q299 1 1–4 + 4Q300 3 1–6) [. . .] everything *2* in order that they may know (the difference) between good and evil and between falsehood and truth, and they may understand [. . .] the mysteries of transgression [. . .] *3* all their wisdom. And they did not know the mystery that is to be/come, and the former things they did not consider. Nor did they know what will come *4* upon them, and their lives they did not save from the mystery that is to be/come.

And this is for you the sign that it is happening: When those begotten of iniquity are delivered up, *5* and wickedness is removed from before righteousness, as darkness is removed from before light, and just as smoke ceases and is no more, so wickedness will cease *6* forever; and righteousness will be revealed as the sun throughout the measure of the world. And all those who cling to the mysteries of wonder will be no more, and knowledge *7* will fill the world, and folly will be there no more.

8 The word is sure to come, and the prophecy is truthful, and from it He will make you know that it is irrevocable. Do not all *9* the nations hate iniquity, and under (it) all of them walk? Does not report of truth (come) from the mouth of all peoples? *10* Is there a lip or tongue that upholds it? What people wishes that one stronger than it should oppress it? Who *11* wishes that his money be stolen by wickedness? And yet what people is there that does not oppress its neighbor?

Where is the nation that has not *12* stolen money belonging to another?

(4Q300 1a ii 1–5/4Q299 2b) *1* [O ma]gicians who teach transgression, say the parable and speak the riddle before it is spoken. And then you will know, if you have looked upon *2* your foolishness. For it has been sealed up from you. Sealed is the vision, and on the eternal mysteries you have not looked, and you have not come to understand knowledge *3* [. . .] for you did not look upon the root of wisdom. And if you open the vision, *4* it will be hidden from you [. . .] all your wisdom for yours is the [. . .] his name, for what is wisdom *5* [. . . st]ill there will not be [. . .].

Exposition

The fragmentary manuscript of the Book of Mysteries from Qumran Cave 1 (1Q27) was among the earliest texts published (Milik and Barthélemy 1955: 102–7). It can now be supplemented by two (4Q299, 300) manuscripts (Schiffman 1993: 203–23; 1994: 206–10; 1995: 207–60) – and perhaps a third (4Q301). Its title is based on the frequent occurrence of the term "mystery" (*rāz*), especially in combination with the verb "be" in the "mystery that is to be/come" (*rāz nihyeh*) – an expression that it shares with Sapiential Work A. Even more clearly than in that work, here the *rāz nihyeh* ("the mystery that is to be/come") is the object of knowledge that pertains to the endtime events.

The most extensive segment is in fact an eschatological scenario (García Martínez 1994: 399–401; Vermes 1995: 272). The full text has been created from fragments of 1Q27 (1 i 1–12), 4Q299 (1 1–4), and 4Q300 (3–16). Though wisdom was given so that humans might be able to distinguish between good and evil and between falsehood and truth, "they did not know the mystery that is to be/come, and the former things they did not consider. Nor did they know what will come upon them, and their lives they did not save from the mystery that is to be/come" (1Q27 1 i 3–4 parallel manuscripts).

The sign that the divine visitation is taking place will be the cessation of wickedness and of the wicked, and the clear revelation of righteousness: "just as smoke ceases and is no more, so wickedness will cease forever; and righteousness will be revealed as the sun throughout the measure of the world" (1Q27 1 i 6–7 parallel manuscripts). The result or aftermath of this visitation is cast in sapiential terms: "knowledge will fill the world, and folly will be there no more" (1Q27 1 i 7 parallel manuscripts).

The eschatological scenario will come to pass when the hypocrisy of the "nations" (Gentiles) becomes manifest. The nations claim to hate iniquity but practice it none the less. They fail to uphold a truthful report, and while protesting oppression they steal from other nations (see 1Q27 1 i 9–12 parallel manuscripts). It is tempting to try to identify the "nations" with the Seleucids or the Romans, but the language is too vague. Nevertheless, it is striking that attention shifts from foolish individuals (within Israel?) at the beginning to the Gentiles taken as a collective at the end.

Another substantial fragment (4Q300 1a ii 1–5; also in 4Q299 2b) challenges "the magicians skilled in transgression" to recite the parable and to relate the riddle before it is spoken. The language is reminiscent of Daniel 2 where King Nebuchadnezzar challenges the magicians to tell him both the dream and its interpretation. There Daniel succeeds where the court magicians failed – because "there is a God in heaven who reveals mysteries, and he has disclosed to King Nebuchadnezzar what will happen at the end of days (Daniel 2:28). The Qumran text issues a harsh judgment against the magicians: "For it has been sealed up from you. Sealed is the vision, and on the eternal mysteries you have not looked, and you have not come to understand knowledge" (4Q300 1 ii 2).

The Cave 4 manuscripts of the Book of Mysteries (4Q299 and 300) do not provide many extensive and coherent blocks of text. In fact, most of the 102 fragments in 4Q299 and of the 14 in 4Q300 seldom contain much more than a few words or phrases. Nevertheless, what can be read helps to give a sense of the major themes.

Creation is acknowledged to be the work of God: "He makes everything [that is to be]. He is from before eternity. Lord is His name, and for eternity . . ." (4Q299 2a + 2c ii 10/4Q300 5). What God has created bears witness to Him: "the lights of the stars for the remembrance of His name . . . the mighty mysteries of light and the ways of darkness . . . the seasons of heat with the times . . ." (4Q299 5 1–3). This lively interest in creation is joined with expectations about God's coming judgment: "it belongs to God to exact vengeance" (4Q299 50 7); "with justice He will contend with . . . against all who transgress His word" (4Q299 56 2–3); "and in His hand is the judgment of them all" (4Q300 11 2).

In the meantime human beings are urged to pursue righteousness and avoid iniquity, especially as exemplified in bearing grudges:

"nothing is more poisonous before Him than one who bears a grudge without . . ." (4Q300 7 2). The exhortations are frequently cast in wisdom terminology: "knowledge . . . understand . . . know . . . discernment . . . understanding . . . intelligence" (4Q299 8 1–8). Nevertheless, there is always the strong sense that true wisdom is the result of divine revelation: "With an abundance of insight He opened our ears so that we might hear" (4Q299 8 6). The mysteries of God are revealed in creation, and yet those who truly understand them receive insight from God that in turn helps them to "do truth and righteousness" and turn away from iniquity.

Much about the Book of Mysteries remains mysterious, especially the precise identity of those who are being criticized and the reason why the hypocrisy of the nations bulks so large in the eschatological scenario. But more important issues are sufficiently clear: the link between morality (good and evil) and wisdom (falsehood and truth), the pivotal role of wisdom in the eschatological scenario, the esoteric nature of this wisdom (which is rejected by the foolish and sealed off from the magicians), and the hope that the divine visitation will take the form of perfect wisdom: "Knowledge will fill the world, and folly will be there no more" (1Q27 1 i 7).

OTHER TEXTS

The text once designated Sapiential Work B (4Q419) may not be a wisdom text at all. Of its eleven fragments only two (1 and 8) are substantial. It was related to Sapiential Work A (1Q26; 4Q415–418, 423) on the basis of the phrase from Deuteronomy 15:7 ("if He [God] will shut His hand, the spirit of all flesh will be removed") that appears in both 4Q416 2 ii 2–3 and 4Q419 8 7. But the style and content of the two works are quite different. Fragment 1 of 4Q419 addresses a plural audience, and exhorts them to act according to the Law of Moses, to respect the eternal priesthood chosen from the seed of Aaron, and to avoid the abomination of impurity. Column 2 of fragment 8 uses third person language to talk about God's visitation, which will mean rewards for the righteous and destruction for the wicked: "to their earth they shall return" (line 8; see Psalm 104:29).

Several other manuscripts from Cave 4 have been designated as sapiential texts on the basis of their vocabulary and content: 4Q307–308, 408, 410–412, 425–426, 472–476, 486–487, and 498. But in all these cases there is not enough running text preserved to make a substantial contribution to our understanding of Qumran wisdom. The work entitled 4Q Songs of the Sage (4Q510–511) is a composition for the *maśkil*, which could refer to a "sage" in general or (what is more likely here, as we have seen elsewhere) to a community official (as in the Community Rule). But the content is more hymnic than sapiential. In it the *maśkil* declares the glory of God shown in creation and Israel's history, warns against the power of demons and other evil spirits, and expresses confidence in God's saving power.

8

"SECTARIAN" WISDOM

INTRODUCTION

The problem of discerning what was a sectarian document at Qumran has been sketched already in the introductory chapter. In the early days of Qumran research there was a tendency to assume that all the nonbiblical texts (even Pseudepigrapha such as 1 Enoch and Jubilees) were "sectarian," that is, they came from the same Jewish sect that produced the works discovered in Qumran Cave 1. Furthermore, there was a host of studies arguing that even works not found at Qumran (for example, ps.-Philo's Biblical Antiquities, Psalms of Solomon, Testaments of the Twelve Patriarchs) were originally Essene compositions.

The pendulum has since moved in the other direction – toward a much narrower definition of what was sectarian at Qumran. Some scholars deny outright that the Qumran writings constituted the library of a religious sect. Others have sought to develop lists of "sectually explicit" features: characteristic terms and ideas, organizational features (the *yaḥad* ["community"], the *maśkil*, the Teacher of Righteousness), composition in Hebrew rather than Aramaic, insistence on the solar calendar, and so forth (Newsom 1990b: 167–87). This effort has yielded a short list of foundational texts that includes the Community Rule, Thanksgiving Hymns, War Scroll, Habakkuk Pesher, Messianic Rule (1QSa), and Damascus Document. The fact that all these texts but the last were found in Qumran Cave 1 suggests that there was something special about the documents in that cave. Since Sapiential Work A and the Book of Mysteries were both represented in Cave 1 (1Q26, 27), it appears that wisdom books were also part of the special "sectarian" collection.

The problem of delineating what was sectarian at Qumran is

complex. Though some texts may have been sectarian in origin, others may have been adopted and approved by the sectarians, and still others may have been kept merely for reference or even refutation. Moreover, it is possible and indeed likely that the Qumran sect was part of a larger and pluriform religious movement in Second Temple Judaism.

We need to return to these issues in the next two chapters, when we consider the significance of the Qumran wisdom texts for our understanding of early Judaism and early Christianity. For our purposes here it seems best to focus on the wisdom elements in two texts that make nearly everyone's list of sectarian documents – the Community Rule (1QS) and the Thanksgiving Hymns (1QH) (Hengel 1974: 218–24; Ringgren 1995; Worrell 1968).

As we have already seen, there are clear links between Qumran wisdom texts and these core sectarian documents. Sapiential Work A (4Q418 55 10) and Thanksgiving Hymns (1QH x 27–28) share a sentence: "According to their knowledge they shall be glorified, each one more than his neighbor." Also, Sapiential Work A and the Book of Mysteries share their characteristic expression "mystery that is to be/come" (*rāz nihyeh*) with 1QS xi 3–4. And so it is legitimate to look for more links between the sectarian documents and the wisdom texts from Qumran.

COMMUNITY RULE (1QS AND 1QSa)

The Community Rule (Leaney 1966), though surely not a wisdom book in itself, does include so many sapiential elements that one can at least talk about wisdom influences or elements in it. A major figure in the work is the *maśkil* – not the musical term of the canonical Psalms but rather the instructor or spiritual guide for the community. The term *maśkil* derives from the Hebrew causative participle "one who makes (another) understand, or become wise." It is part of the standard wisdom vocabulary in the Hebrew Bible and related works.

One way to read the Community Rule is to regard it as a handbook or instruction manual for the community's spiritual director, the *maśkil* (Newsom 1990a: 373–82). This approach, already suggested from the Qumran Cave manuscript (1QS), has been confirmed and extended by fragments of the work found in Cave 4. For example, the lengthy instruction in 1QS v 1–20 about "the men of the Torah who have dedicated themselves to turn from all evil and to hold fast to all that he has commanded" is prefaced in 4QS B (= 4Q256) 5 1 and 4QS D (= 4Q258) 1 i 1 by the phrase "Instruction (midrash) for the *maśkil* concerning. . . ."

The most famous part of the Community Rule is the "Instruction on the Two Spirits" (iii 13–iv 26). It is presented to the *maśkil* as a set piece by which he can instruct all the sons of light concerning "the nature of all the sons of men, according to all the kinds of spirits they possess, the signs identifying their works during their lifetimes, and their visitation for chastisement, along with the times of their reward" (iii 13–15). The cosmic and eschatological framework laid out in the instruction provides the "sons of light" with a map of the moral universe and thus gives them perfect wisdom.

The moral map is clear and simple. From "the God of knowledge" (a frequent epithet in Sapiential Work A) "comes all that is and shall be" – a statement that safeguards the sovereignty of God. But the God of knowledge has placed over humankind two spirits, represented by the Prince of Light and the Angel of Darkness. The children of light, led by the Prince of Light, do the deeds of light, whereas the children of darkness, led by the Angel of Darkness, do the deeds of darkness (Duhaime 1987: 32–56; 1988: 401–22). All this continues until the visitation: "In the mysteries of His understanding, and in His glorious wisdom, God has ordained an end for iniquity, and at the time of the visitation He will destroy it forever" (iv 18–19).

Much of the instruction concerns the virtues and good deeds that should characterize the children of light, and the vices and evil deeds that characterize the children of darkness, along with the rewards and punishments that await both groups at the "visitation." Meanwhile, there is a struggle in the hearts of humans between the spirits of truth and falsehood (iv 23). One's reward or punishment depends on whether one's "lot in their two divisions is great or small" (iv 16).

This kind of cosmic, eschatological, and moral framework is presupposed (at least in part) in some of the Qumran wisdom texts. Its full form in the Community Rule at least gives coherence to those texts. Whether some form of the instruction antedated the Qumran wisdom texts or is a synthesis of them, is difficult to decide.

The "Hymn of Praise" that concludes the Community Rule (x 9–xi 22), which may also be intended for the *maśkil,* celebrates the wisdom that comes from divine revelation: "For my light has sprung from the source of His knowledge; my eyes have beheld His marvelous deeds, and the light of my heart is in the mystery to be/come" (xi 3–4). The latter expression "the mystery to be/come" (*rāz nihyeh*) is familiar from Sapiential Work A and may refer to something like the instruction in iii 13–iv 26. The wisdom that the speaker has obtained is a gift from God (and thus a revelation), and concerns the mysteries of the universe. The hymn of praise is rounded off with a blessing: "Blessed are You, my God, who opens the heart of Your servant to knowledge" (xi 15–16).

The appendix to the Community Rule, or the Messianic Rule (1QSa), stipulates that young men up to the age of twenty shall be instructed in the "Book of Meditation" – a term alluded to previously in 4Q417 2 i 13–18. Since Sapiential Work A refers to that book as another book, it can hardly be the same as Sapiential Work A. It does appear, however, that study of a text with wisdom elements in it (the "Book of Meditation") was part of the spiritual formation of prospective members of the group.

The most famous part of the Messianic Rule (1QSa) is the description of the "messianic banquet" (ii 11–22) in which the community's meal in the present prepares for and reflects the heavenly banquet at which the Messiah of Aaron (the Priest) and the Messiah of Israel (a David figure) play prominent roles. According to Psalm 154, the appropriate topics of conversation for the community of the righteous as they eat and drink together are wisdom and the Torah: "When they eat in fullness, she is mentioned; and when they drink in community together, their meditation is on the Law of the Most High" (11Q5 xviii 11–12). Likewise, Psalm 154's motif of the sacrifice of praise ("one who glorifies the Most High He accepts as one who brings a meal offering," 7–8) is paralleled by 1QS ix 4–5: "And the offering of the lips shall be like an acceptable fragrance of righteousness, and perfection of way like a delectable free-will offering."

THANKSGIVING HYMNS (1QH)

The Thanksgiving Hymns (or, Hodayot) constitute one of the longest and most important documents among the Qumran scrolls (Holm-Nielsen 1960; Kittel 1981). These hymns usually begin with a confessional formula ("I thank Thee, O Lord") found in the Hebrew Bible (see also Matthew 11:25; Luke 10:21). They use some elements from the biblical thanksgiving psalms (descriptions of distress and rescue from it, confessions of God's saving power, expressions of praise of and gratitude to God). But they depart from the biblical script by omitting references to Temple sacrifices, by stringing together phrases from various biblical books (the "anthological" style), and by adopting what often appears to be a rambling logic. These hymns present many problems of interpretation, of which the two most important are the identity of the speaker and the life-setting. Was the speaker ("I") the Teacher of Righteousness, the whole community taken collectively, or some (or any) member of it? Were these hymns used in community worship or for private meditation?

Though not a wisdom document in itself, the Thanksgiving Hymns contain many wisdom elements (Tanzer 1987). Indeed the work provides evidence for the sect's assimilation of wisdom terminology and conceptuality into its own world view. The speaker reflects on God's wisdom at work in creation: "By Your wisdom You established eternal [. . .] and before creating them You knew all their works for ever and ever" (ix [= i] 7–8). He also envisions perfect union with God as being "illumined with perfect light for ever."

The wisdom vocabulary in the Thanksgiving Hymns is sporadic, only one element in a larger literary tapestry. Nevertheless, there are verbal and thematic links between the Thanksgiving Hymns and Sapiential Work A. Especially noteworthy is the occurrence of the same phrase "according to their knowledge they shall be glorified, each one more than his neighbor" in both 1QH x 27–28 and 4Q418 55 10. This coincidence could be explained in various ways: the use of Sapiential Work A in the Thanksgiving Hymns, the use of Thanksgiving Hymns by Sapiential Text A, or the common use of a cliché. At any rate, the phrase does show a link between the wisdom text and a "sectarian" text.

The wisdom language in Thanksgiving Hymns is most prominent in three contexts: creation, revelation, and the role of the speaker ("I"). The speaker reflects on God's wisdom in creating heaven and earth, and in forming "the spirit of man": "In the wisdom of Your knowledge You did establish their destiny before they were" (i 19–20). The very structure of the universe has been shaped by the wisdom of God: "Without it nothing is nor shall be, for the God of knowledge has established it" (xii 10–11). Such expressions, of course, are based on the Hebrew Bible and are not especially innovative. Moreover, the level of the "personification" of Wisdom in the text is low.

The most prominent context for wisdom language in the

Thanksgiving Hymns is revelation. This is based on a sober appreciation of human weakness: "Behold, [I was taken] from dust [and]
fashioned [out of clay] as a source of uncleanness and a shameful
nakedness, a heap of dust . . ." (xi 24–25). This low estimate of
human nature (which appears often in the Thanksgiving Hymns) is
balanced by celebration of the precious gift of knowledge from
God: "I [thank You, O Lord], for You have enlightened me through
Your truth. In Your marvelous mysteries, and in Your loving kind-
ness to a man [of vanity, and] in the greatness of Your mercy to a
perverse heart You have granted me knowledge" (vii 26–27).
Wisdom for the Qumran sectarians derives chiefly from divine revelation, and not so much from empirical observation of creation and
human relations.

The speaker ("I") claims to have been the special recipient of
wisdom from God: "You have revealed Yourself to me in Your
power . . . through me You have illumined the face of the congregation" (iv 23, 27). The speaker here (and elsewhere) appears to be a
mediator between God and the heavenly court on the one hand, and
the community on the other hand. Even the sufferings of the speaker are attributed to the wisdom of God: "for it is according to the
mystery of Your wisdom that You have rebuked me" (ix 23). The interpretation of the speaker as the Teacher of Righteousness makes
good sense out of such statements. If that interpretation is correct,
then the Teacher of Righteousness would be at least in part a
wisdom teacher – at least to the extent of using wisdom language
and concepts to explain his sufferings and his role within the
movement.

Thus, the "wisdom" sections of the Thanksgiving Hymns make
three basic points: God's wisdom created the world and humankind.
The best and only real wisdom for humans is the wisdom that God
gives (divine revelation). The speaker ("I") is a privileged recipient
of God's gift of wisdom and must pass that wisdom on to others.

9

WISDOM TEXTS FROM QUMRAN AND EARLY JUDAISM

INTRODUCTION

Thus far I have offered translations and expositions of the major wisdom writings found at Qumran. In doing so I have tried to respect the particularity of each of the texts and to bring out their distinctive literary and theological emphases. In this synthetic chapter, it would be improper exegetical methodology to mix all these texts together to describe "the Qumran understanding of wisdom" and relate it to early Judaism as if both were unitary phenomena. Moreover, such a procedure would run into the larger problems of the nature of the Qumran library and of the identity of the people who settled there.

Yet it is proper and legitimate to bring together some unifying threads and themes, and thus to call attention to the wider significance that the Qumran wisdom texts may have. I shall consider in turn their significance for the study of the Hebrew Bible and early Judaism, as well as of the Qumran community.

THE HEBREW BIBLE AND EARLY JUDAISM

Much of what is found in the Qumran wisdom texts fits well with the wisdom books of the Hebrew Bible and early Judaism, especially Sirach and 1 Enoch. The chief contribution of the Qumran texts is to expand the repertoire of the literary forms and the contents of Jewish wisdom texts from the Second Temple period. Thanks to the Qumran wisdom documents we now have more data with which to work in both form and content. The most important additions appear in the areas of form and content.

The most prominent literary genre among the Qumran wisdom

texts is the instruction or admonition in which the sage instructs either an individual or a group – and sometimes both. The most extensive instruction appears in Sapiential Work A (1Q26; 4Q415–418, 423). But several other texts (1Q27/4Q299–300; 4Q185, 298, 413, 420–421, 424, 525) also use the instruction format. Within these larger instructions, there are the frequent calls to pay attention ("my son . . . understanding child . . . listen to me . . . you are poor") as well as the use of smaller forms such as the beatitude (4Q185, 525).

Also prominent among the Qumran wisdom texts are poems and hymns: the Hymn to the Creator (11Q5 xxvi 9–15), Psalm 154, Sirach 51, and the Hymn of Knowledge (4Q413). These works either speak about wisdom in a broader context or celebrate Wisdom as a personal figure. Whether the description of Lady Folly in 4Q184 should be classified as a poem or an instruction is not entirely clear.

With regard to content, the best preserved parts of Sapiential Work A (1Q26; 4Q415–418, 423) deal with topics that are familiar on the agenda of the sages: money and possessions, social relations, and family matters. Two of the smaller sapiential works (4Q420–421, 424) describe the kinds of persons to be avoided and those who are to be sought out as friends and emissaries.

The "beatitudes" in 4Q525 and 4Q185 describe what constitutes happiness for human beings. The "happy" person is wise, and the wise person is righteous, and the righteous person follows the lead of the Torah. That point – common in Jewish wisdom writings – is made several times in the "beatitude" texts. Moreover, in Sapiential Work A there are cases in which biblical texts – the laws about annuling a wife's vows (Numbers 30:6–15) and about "mixed things" (Leviticus 19:19; Deuteronomy 22:9–11) – are used in the context of a wisdom instruction. As in Sirach, there is a tendency at points to join the sapiential and halakhic traditions. This association leads in turn to a tendency to equate the Torah with the figure of Wisdom (see 4Q185, 525).

The portrayal of Wisdom as a personal figure in the tradition of Proverbs 8 and Sirach 24 is found also in some Qumran texts, though not as vividly as in the biblical texts. In the Hymn to the Creator, Wisdom or Knowledge plays a role in creation. In Sirach 51 Wisdom is the object of the speaker's search. It must be admitted, however, that Lady Folly is described in 4Q184 more graphically than Lady Wisdom.

As in biblical wisdom writings (especially Sirach), creation is frequently the horizon against which the wise person acts. Nevertheless, some of the Qumran wisdom texts seem far more interested in the future eschatological judgment as the horizon for ethical activity than in the past or the present of creation. A typical warning about God's judgment appears in 4Q417 1 i 15–17: "For before the wrath of His anger none will stand. And who will be declared righteous when He gives judgment? And without forgiveness, how will there stand before Him any poor man?"

Perhaps the most striking contribution of the Qumran wisdom texts is their insistence on wisdom as a gift from God and on the need for understanding the "mystery that is to be/come." According to Psalm 154, "wisdom is given to make known the glory of God." According to 4Q185, "God gave her to Israel, and with a good measure He measures her out."

There is a special wisdom to be found in studying the "mystery that is to be/come" – a topic prominent in Sapiential Work A and the Book of Mysteries. The "mystery" appears to be a body of teaching that involves creation, ethical activity, and eschatology. Though creation is an element, translations such as the "mystery of being" or the "mystery of existence" seem too metaphysical and static. From its parallel phrases this mystery appears to be associated with the knowledge of righteousness and iniquity ("all the ways of truth ... all the roots of iniquity," 4Q416 2 iii 14), and also with eschatology ("the birth-time of salvation, and who is to inherit glory and iniquity," 4Q417 1 i 10–11).

It is difficult to identify precisely what the "mystery that is to be/come" is. It may be something like the teaching about the Two Spirits in 1QS iii–iv. At any rate, in some Qumran wisdom writings it seems to have the status of a special revelation, a privileged communication about God's working in the world and the appropriate response of wise and righteous persons to it.

The representation of women is generally what one might expect in Jewish wisdom writings. Lady Folly is depicted in 4Q184 in lurid detail as a seductress eager to ruin prospective sages. Sapiential Work A insists on the husband's God-given authority over his wife (4Q416 2 iv). The most distinctive contribution of the Qumran wisdom texts to our understanding of the role of women comes in what appears to be an instruction directed to a woman in 4Q415 2 ii 1–9. Although the advice proceeds from patriarchal assumptions and is quite conventional in content, the very fact that a woman is directly addressed in a Jewish wisdom instruction is itself surprising.

QUMRAN COMMUNITY

In the introductory chapter, I stated my views on the nature of the Qumran library and community. The Qumran scrolls are, I believe, the remnants of the library of a Jewish religious sect (most likely Essenes) that had a center at Qumran from the second century BCE to the first century CE. Despite challenges from many directions, this approach remains the most plausible and widely held theory about the Dead Sea scrolls found at Qumran (Talmon 1994: 3–24). In the preceding chapter I pointed out some close links between the wisdom writings from Qumran and two of the works – Rule of the Community (1QS and 1QSa) and Thanksgiving Hymns (1QH) – regarded as most representative of the thinking and life of the Qumran sect. The peculiar phrase "the mystery that is to be/come" so characteristic of Sapiential Work A and the Book of Mysteries also appears in 1QS xi 3–4. And there is a direct verbal overlap between 4Q418 55 10 and 1QH x 27–28, as well as many linguistic parallels between the Qumran wisdom books and the more definitely sectarian works.

If the conventional approach to the Qumran library and community is accepted, then it is easy to suppose that much in the Qumran wisdom corpus would be at home in the Qumran community. The description of the wisdom community and its sacrifice of praise in Psalm 154, the warnings against Lady Folly in 4Q184, the eschatological scenarios of judgment in 4Q185 and Sapiential Work A, the dualistic language scattered throughout the works, the extensive use of the instruction form – all these features and more would fit nicely with what we know about the Qumran sect.

And yet there are other elements in the Qumran wisdom texts that do not fit the isolated and (some say) monastic conditions of Qumran. The chief topics in the best preserved parts of Sapiential Work A are commercial transactions (loans and deposits), social relations (with superiors and inferiors), and family matters (wife, parents, in-laws). These topics presuppose a secular setting in which the person being instructed is a participant in Jewish life – and not someone living under the strictures of the Community Rule (1QS). Likewise, 4QProverbs (4Q424) describes the kinds of persons that a wise man will best avoid. The one being instructed engages in lawsuits and has business dealings. He has authority over money and possessions, and can and must delegate his authority to others. Again this advice presupposes a setting quite different from that of the Community Rule. Furthermore, none of the Qumran wisdom texts is so "sectarian" by the narrow standards of 1QS and 1QH as to demand a Qumran origin or a use only in the Qumran setting.

So on the one hand, there are clear links between some Qumran wisdom texts and the Qumran sect. And on the other hand, much of the Qumran wisdom material presupposes a life-setting quite different from what we imagine to have existed at the Qumran settlement.

How is this situation to be explained? What does it tell us about Second Temple Judaism? One possibility is that the Qumran wisdom texts are merely "books in a library" – regarded only as edifying reading. But the fact that there are six fragmentary manuscripts of Sapiential Work A (1Q26; 4Q415–418, 423) argues against such a minimalist explanation.

More likely, the Qumran wisdom writings (or, at least some of them) represent the intellectual and religious heritage of a larger movement within Second Temple Judaism. If the movement was Essene, we know from ancient sources that there were different ways of being an Essene. The Qumran branch (*yaḥad*) may have been a break-away Essene faction, a "strict observance" group that contested the Maccabean usurpation of the high priesthood. Or the Qumran community may have served as a renewal center or a spiritual-life center for the wider Essene movement.

From the Damascus Document in particular we know of another way of being a member of the (Essene?) movement. Fragments of this work, already known from two manuscripts discovered in the Cairo Geniza in the late nineteenth century, were found in Qumran Caves 4, 5, and 6. The statutes in columns 9 through 16 presuppose a life-setting in which members live in "camps" or communes, marry and bear children, and have property and money. These rules may have applied to a group or lifestyle different from those envisioned in the Community Rule. Or they may reflect a pre-Qumranic phase in the movement's history.

Though not a wisdom book, the Damascus Document does use wisdom terminology (Denis 1967), especially in the exhortations that constitute the first part of the book: "God loves knowledge. Wisdom and understanding He has set before Him, and prudence and knowledge serve Him" (ii 2–3). The Qumran wisdom writings may offer further illumination on the broader Jewish movement from which the Qumran library and sect emerged. They may show us more about the secular style of being an Essene that we glimpse in the Damascus Document and that may have antedated what is set forth in the Community Rule.

10

WISDOM TEXTS FROM QUMRAN AND EARLY CHRISTIANITY

INTRODUCTION

I regard the Qumran/Essene movement and the Jesus/earliest church movement as independent and parallel phenomena within late Second Temple Judaism. Though John the Baptist may have had ties to the Essenes and some Essenes may have become Christians, I doubt that there was much direct influence from the Essenes (who are never mentioned in the New Testament) on Jesus and the earliest Christians. The Qumran scrolls are important for the study of early Christianity mainly because they tell us about the language, theological concepts, and organizational structures of a Palestinian Jewish group active from the second century BCE to the first century CE. They provide good parallels; but they are not the sources for the New Testament.

PARTICULAR PASSAGES

The Qumran wisdom texts illumine some particular New Testament passages. The series of at least five beatitudes in 4Q525 2 ii parallel in form the series of beatitudes in Matthew 5:3–12 and Luke 6:20–23. They differ in content since the Qumran beatitudes are oriented toward wisdom and the "Law of the Most High" whereas the New Testament beatitudes look toward the eschatological kingdom of God and hold out the possibility of suffering "on my account" (Matt 5:12) or "on account of the Son of Man" (Luke 6:22). This is a case where the parallel serves also to highlight an important difference.

Sapiential Work A may help us to understand two Pauline texts better. 4Q416 2 ii 21 refers to a wife as a "vessel" (*kělî*): "And moreover do not dishonor the vessel of your bosom (or, your lawful vessel)." Paul appears to use similar language with regard to a wife in 1 Thessalonians 4:4 when he speaks of each acquiring or keeping his own *skeuos* (Greek for "vessel") in holiness and honor. In the context of punishment by flogging in 4Q417 1 i 27, there may be a reference to thirty-nine strokes as a punishment as in 2 Corinthians 11:24: "Five times I have received from the Jews the forty lashes minus one." It must be admitted, however, that only the "nine" is legible in the Qumran text and that "thirty" has been supplied on the basis of 2 Corinthians 11:24.

JESUS AND WISDOM

The most important general contributions of the Qumran wisdom texts to New Testament studies lie in their extending what we know about wisdom teaching and wisdom teachers in Jesus' time (Witherington 1994).

That Jesus was to some extent a wisdom teacher is clear from even a cursory look at the Gospels. He uses the forms typically employed by wisdom teachers (Perdue 1986: 3–35; Piper 1989; Winton 1990) such as Ben Sira and in the Qumran wisdom texts. He employs the familiar Hebrew poetic device of parallelism to say the same thing either in synonymous terms (see Mark 3:24–25) or in antithetical terms (see Matt 12:35). He uses proverbs: "No one can serve two masters" (Matt 6:22). He makes comparisons and tells parables: "The kingdom of heaven is like a treasure . . . a merchant . . . a net" (Matt 13:44–50). He asks questions: "Can anyone of you by worrying add a single hour to your span of life?" (Matt 6:27). He sprinkles his teaching with beatitudes: "Blessed are those who hear the word of God and obey it" (Luke 11:28). He gives admonitions: "Be on your guard against all kinds of greed; for one's life does not consist in abundance of possessions" (Luke 12:15). And large sections of his teachings take the form of wisdom instructions (Matt 5–7; Luke 6:20–49; 11:9–13).

Although much of Jesus' teaching in the Synoptic tradition corresponds with the form and content of the wisdom tradition found in Jewish wisdom books in general and in the Qumran wisdom writings in particular, there is an uncommonly ironical or paradoxical element to it that calls into question the assumptions and values that most people hold. In Luke 6:20 Jesus calls the poor "blessed" or "happy" or even "fortunate" – depending on what translation one uses. He promises that "those who want to save their life will lose it, and those who lose their life for my sake and for the sake of the gospel will save it" (Mark 8:35). He claims that "the last will be first and the first last" (Matt 20:16). These paradoxical sayings seem to defy logic, or at least cause the listeners to rethink their assumptions about life. Such provocative sayings are called aphorisms.

Calling the Jesus of the Synoptic Gospels a teacher does not exclude the descriptions of him as an eschatological prophet or as a charismatic healer. Ben Sira, who is perhaps the best known wisdom teacher of Second Temple Judaism, was also an interpreter of Scripture and an enthusiastic supporter of the Temple priesthood (and perhaps even from a priestly family).

The Qumran wisdom texts provide further evidence for the literary forms used by wisdom teachers in Jesus' time and the topics that concerned them. However, they lack the radical and paradoxical character of some of Jesus' wisdom teachings. They do not call the poor "blessed" or "happy," though some texts do stress the need to face the poverty that goes with the human condition and/or that is involved in one's state of life. They do not speak about losing one's life to save it or about the last being first and the first being last. They lack the ironic or aphoristic quality that marks much of Jesus' wisdom.

The prominence of the wisdom instruction genre at Qumran is especially important for understanding the New Testament's "ethical teachings." The wisdom instructor imparts advice on how to live and what to think. The wisdom instruction is not a collection of proverbs as in Proverbs 10–22 but rather an address in the style found in Proverbs 1–9 and 22–24 and in Sirach. The setting is direct address, and the advice moves from topic to topic rather quickly. It is possible to class as wisdom instructions the sayings source Q shared by Matthew and Luke, some of the Matthean discourses (especially the Sermon on the Mount), the letter of James, and the paraenetic sections of the Pauline epistles – those passages most often used in Christian moral teaching.

The wisdom of Jesus according to the Synoptic Gospels has a strong note of eschatology. The kingdom of God, though inaugurated or anticipated in Jesus' life and ministry, is still future in its fullness. Yet despite its prominence in Jesus' preaching, the kingdom of God remains elusive and ill-defined. Nevertheless, perceiving the importance of the kingdom of God in the present and acting upon it (see Matt 13:44–46) is the key to wisdom and happiness. In certain Qumran wisdom texts – Sapiential Work A and the Book of Mysteries – the "mystery that is to be/come" (*rāz nihyeh*) plays an analogous role. Its content is assumed rather than defined or described in detail. Its importance is emphasized by recurrent calls to study it, meditate upon it, and so forth. It is the key to knowing God's future plans and to a wise and happy life in the present.

The portrayal of Wisdom as a (female) personal figure in the Hymn to the Creator (weakly) and Sirach 51 (strongly) provides further background to the process by which Jesus the wisdom teacher became the incarnate Wisdom of God. Likewise, the tendency to identify Wisdom and the Torah (see 4Q185; 4Q525) contributes to this development. Some sayings in the Q tradition (see Luke 7:35; 11:49–50) present Jesus as an emissary of Wisdom, while in other Q sayings (see Luke 13:34/Matthew 23:37; Luke 10:22/Matthew 11:27) Jesus seems to take on the persona of Wisdom. Then in the tradition of Proverbs 8, Sirach 24, and Wisdom 7, the earliest Christian hymns (Colossians 1:15–20; Hebrews 1:3; John 1:1–18) celebrate Jesus as the Wisdom of God. The portrayal of Jesus both as a wisdom teacher and as the Wisdom of God is especially prominent in the Gospels of Matthew (Byrskog 1994; Deutsch 1987; Suggs 1970) and John (Scott 1992; Willett 1992). The Qumran wisdom texts are not nearly as important as the biblical texts are in discerning the process by which Jesus the wisdom teacher became the Wisdom of God. But they do give us more data for appreciating the person of Wisdom and her/his relation to the Torah.

TWO CONTROVERSIES

The Qumran wisdom texts also deserve some attention in two areas of debate among New Testament scholars: the (first) sapiential stratum in Q, and Jesus as a Cynic philosopher.

According to some scholars (Kloppenborg 1987; Mack 1993), it is possible to isolate a wisdom instruction as the earliest stratum of Q. This wisdom instruction dealt with true happiness, love of enemies, avoiding hypocrisy, the relation between words and deeds, the simple lifestyle, confidence in God's care, dealing with anxiety, the kingdom of God, and the true followers of Jesus. According to some, the primitive sapiential stratum was then expanded and transformed by apocalyptic material.

The Qumran wisdom texts can neither prove nor disprove the

hypothesis about the earliest stage in the literary and theological history of the Q source. But they do suggest that wisdom teachings from first-century Palestine most likely had a strong mixture of sapiential and apocalyptic material. To isolate the sapiential elements from the apocalyptic elements and then to reconstruct the wisdom instruction shorn of apocalypticism does not fit with what we know about wisdom teachings from Qumran and elsewhere in first-century Palestine.

That Jesus may have looked like a Cynic philosopher to some of his contemporaries (Crossan 1991; Downing 1992; Vaage 1994; Betz 1994: 453–75) is not entirely implausible. The themes of Jesus' teaching – voluntary poverty, severance of family ties, the renunciation of needs, and carefree and fearless attitudes toward life – have parallels in reports about Cynic philosophers. Likewise, Jesus' use of irony and paradox, as well as his reliance on symbolic actions, may have caused his Palestinian contemporaries to look upon him as something like a Cynic philosopher – who was a common phenomenon in the Greco-Roman world (and that included Palestine!).

Again the Qumran wisdom texts can neither prove nor disprove the Jesus as Cynic hypothesis. But they do point to the existence of a more traditional style of Jewish wisdom activity in first-century Palestine. And they raise further questions. Why should we search for parallels and analogies far removed in time and place when we have some impressive evidence for Jewish wisdom movements in late Second Temple times? And why should we not better attribute the distinctive style and tone of the wisdom teachings in the Gospels to the religious genius of Jesus?

CONCLUSION

This introduction to the wisdom texts from Qumran has focused on the most substantial and important manuscripts. The translations and literary analyses have shown how these Jewish wisdom documents communicated and illustrated what their authors considered to be important. As we have seen, these texts represent a rich mixture of literary forms and theological perspectives.

This examination of the biggest and best preserved wisdom texts from Qumran is only a beginning. Much remains for researchers in the years to come: joining and analyzing the scraps of texts called "sapiential," identifying small fragments and integrating them into larger units, searching for further links between Qumran wisdom texts and other Jewish wisdom writings (Sirach, 1 Enoch, etc.), using the wisdom texts to help resolve the puzzles associated with the Qumran sect and its library, and contributing to our understanding of the world of Jesus (the "Wisdom of God") and the early Christians.

The discovery of the Qumran scrolls from 1947 onward has been appropriately described as the most important archaeological discovery ever. And the slowness of their publication has been called the academic scandal of the century. These are fascinating stories in themselves. Yet to concentrate on the scientific and academic aspects of these texts to the exclusion of their content is to miss their point. The wisdom texts from Qumran challenge readers in the late twentieth and early twenty-first century to take seriously the humanistic and theological values of their authors: their devotion to knowledge and wisdom, their insistence on the relation between wisdom and righteous action, and their recognition that creation belongs to God and we live and act within the unfolding plan of God – the mystery that is to be/come. They challenge us to make our own the words of Sirach 51:18 preserved in the Cave 11 Psalms Scroll: "I resolved and delighted in her, and I was zealous for good, and I shall not turn back."

Appendix

THE BEN SIRA SCROLL
FROM MASADA

INTRODUCTION

The term "Dead Sea scrolls" applies not only to Qumran but also to discoveries in several other sites in the general area. One of the places that is often included under this heading is Masada, first a villa complex built by Herod the Great and then the Jewish fortress where the First Jewish Revolt ended in 73/74 CE. In 1965 the famous Israeli general/archaeologist/biblical-scholar/politician Yigael Yadin published (Yadin 1965) a manuscript discovered at Masada in 1964 that contained large fragments of the book of Ben Sira (also known in its Greek version as Sirach or Ecclesiasticus) in the original Hebrew version of the work. The fragments cover from 39:27 through 43:30, which is a fairly substantial section of a very long (51 chapters) book.

The book of Sirach is canonical Scripture in the Catholic and Orthodox churches, and is well known also in the Protestant and Jewish traditions (Skehan and Di Lella 1987). Its main version for almost 2,000 years has been the Greek text contained in the Septuagint. On it the Latin and (to some extent) Syriac versions depend. But as the prologue to the Greek version makes clear, the book was composed in Hebrew and translated into Greek by the grandson of the author. Even the grandson admitted that between the Hebrew and the Greek there is "no small difference." The Greek translation was made in Egypt around 120 BCE, and the original Hebrew must have been composed around 180 BCE in Jerusalem where its author – usually called Ben Sira (see 50:27) – ran some kind of school for prospective sages.

In 1896 and thereafter, parts of the Hebrew text of Sirach were recovered from the Cairo Geniza, a repository for discarded Jewish manuscripts. The manuscripts are medieval. The largest and most important is known as MS B, which contains the main text of large sections of Sirach as well as marginal notations. Although some scholars rejected the Cairo Geniza fragments of Sirach as retranslations into Hebrew and therefore as textually unimportant, other scholars recognized (correctly) that the Geniza fragments represent in large part the original Hebrew version from antiquity. Yet even the champions of the authenticity of MS B admitted the presence of some later (even medieval) elements. Many of the marginal notes in MS B were supposed (correctly) to have been textual variants from other Sirach manuscripts, something like the critical apparatus printed at the foot of the pages in modern critical editions of ancient texts.

The Masada Sirach manuscript clearly antedated 73/74 CE, when the Romans overran the Jewish garrison there. Analysis of the script (paleography) indicated an even earlier date of origin – in the first half of the first century BCE. So now we have a Hebrew manuscript of Sirach 39:27–43:30 that was copied within a hundred years or so of the work's original composition.

Study of the Masada Sirach manuscript has vindicated the basic antiquity and reliability of MS B with which it shares a large portion of text. It also confirms that the marginal notes do indeed contain ancient textual variants. The Masada manuscript used critically along with MS B and its marginal notes and the Greek version enables us to get fairly close to the Hebrew text as written by Ben Sira of Jerusalem, and can help us to understand better the Greek translation (and its dependent Latin version) as well as the Syriac version (which depends for the most part on the Hebrew tradition and only occasionally on the Greek). Thus the discovery of the Ben Sira scroll at Masada has greatly clarified the textual history of this long and important Jewish wisdom book.

Nevertheless, one cannot simply describe the Masada Sirach scroll as the original text. The textual situation is more complicated, as the following three examples will illustrate. These three passages contain some of the best preserved parts of the Masada Ben Sira manuscript: the instruction about shame (41:15–42:8), the hymn about God's glory in creation (42:15–25), and the beginning of the "praise of famous men" (44:1–17).

The first example will show that the Masada Ben Sira manuscript both agrees and disagrees with the other ancient textual witnesses, and so one cannot rely on it alone to provide the original Hebrew text and disregard all the other textual evidence. The second example calls attention to a very important contribution of the Masada Ben Sira manuscript in providing the Hebrew text for verses that were previously known from the Greek version. Even here, however, the Hebrew text raises questions about the textual basis and/or the competency of the Greek translation. The third example will show that even the earliest and best manuscript contains some errors.

Establishing the text of Sirach is one of the most difficult tasks in biblical studies. The translator of or commentator on Sirach today is always faced with the problem of deciding what should be the basis for the translation or commentary. Should it be the (canonical at least in Catholic and Orthodox traditions) Greek text throughout? Should it be the Hebrew fragments (which cover large parts of the work) supplemented by the Greek version where there is no Hebrew? Or should it be the Greek as corrected and improved by the Hebrew fragments? This in turn raises the question as to whose book – that of Ben Sira of Jerusalem, or that of his grandson in Egypt, or that of the modern editor? – is being translated and interpreted, and in some religious traditions accepted as Holy Scripture.

In the following translations of texts from Sirach according to the Masada manuscript, the first double number refers to the traditional chapter and verse (41:15), and the second number (after the slash) to the line in the column of the Masada manuscript (18). In the Masada manuscript the lines are arranged by stichs, that is, in sense lines that bring out the parallelism that is generally Ben Sira's principle of composition. The same kind of arrangement occurs in some Qumran manuscripts of Proverbs (4Q102–103) and Sirach (2Q18). Thus in most cases the traditional chapter-and-verse numbers correspond to the line numbers in the Masada manuscript.

TEXT 1: ON SHAME (SIRACH 41:15–42:8 = MASADA iii 18–iv 15)

Text

41:15/iii 18 An instruction about shame hear, O children [. . ., and put] to shame according to my rules. *41:16/19* Not all shame is shameful, and not all humiliation is chosen.

41:17/20 Be ashamed before father and mother of wantonness; before ruler and prince of falsehood; *41:18/21* before master and mistress of conspiracy, before congregation and people of [. . c]rime; *41:18c–19a/22* before associate and neighbor of wrongdoing, before the place you sojourn of [. . . t]heft; *41:19bc/23* of breaking an oath or covenant, and of stretching out an elbow over food, *41:19d and 21a/24* of refus-[ing] to grant a request, and of turning aside your kin, *41:21b and 20a/25* of withholding an allotted share, of asking a greeting of a deaf-mute, *41:21c and 20b/iv 1* of gazing at a [married woman], and of thinking about a foreign woman, *41:22ab/2* of oppressing a ser[vant gir]l of yours, and of raising yourself upon her bed; *41:22cd/3* before a loved one of shameful words, and before a stranger of giving reproach; *42:1/4* of repeating a word you hear, and of laying bare every word of counsel. *42:1cd/5* And be ashamed in truth, and find favor in the eyes of every living being.

42:1ef/6 [Bu]t do not be ashamed of these, and do not respect persons and sin: *42:2/7* of the Law of the Most High and the precept, and of justice to make righteous the wicked; *42:3/8* of the account of an associate and a wayfarer, and of dividing an inheritance and property; *42:4a and 5a/9* of dusting scales and a balance, and of polishing a weight and a stone; *42:4b* of acquiring much or little, [. . .] of bartering about a merchant's wares; *42:5bc/11* and [of much chastisement upon children], and upon an evil servant plus a flogged back. *42:6/12* Set a seal [upon a woman who plays the] fool, and where there are many hands a key; *42:7/13* of [. . . on] a deposit a number, and of what [. . .] and given out everything in writing; *42:8/14* of [. . .] and a fool, and of a tottering old [man] occupied with fornication. *42:8cd/15* And you will be truly enlightened, and [. . .] before every living being.

Exposition

After a call to pay attention and distinguish between things of which one should be ashamed and not be ashamed (41:15–16), Ben Sira lists shameful actions and the persons before whom one should be ashamed to do them (41:17–42:1d). Then he lists things of which one should not be ashamed (42:1e–8). Knowing how to distinguish between what does and what does not bring shame leads to a "good name" for the sage. This kind of practical advice is typical of what appears in the body of the book of Sirach. And Sirach, of course, is the longest and best example of the wisdom instruction genre that is so well represented by the wisdom instructions treated in Chapters 5, 6, and 7 in this book.

The order in which the advice about shame is given in the Masada manuscript is slightly different and superior to the order presupposed in the Greek tradition (on which the traditional numeration of verses is based). With regard to the other Hebrew witnesses (MS B and the marginal notes) for Sirach 41:15–42:8, the Masada text for this section gives evidence for a variety of agreements. In Sirach 41:17 the Masada manuscript and the marginal note in MS B agree in using the rare Hebrew word *paḥaz* ("wantonness") that appears only once in the Hebrew Bible (see Genesis 49:4) whereas MS B uses the far more common term *zĕnût* ("fornication"). The more difficult word *paḥaz* is more likely the original reading, and *zĕnût* appears to have been an easier substitute. But note that the Greek version reads *porneia* (= Hebrew *zĕnût*), which suggests that the substitution may have occurred early in the textual transmission.

In Sirach 41:21a (= line iii 24) the Masada manuscript reads "of turning aside your kin." It agrees first with MS B and the Greek with the verb "turning aside" against the corrupt reading "of saving" in the margin of MS B. Then in the noun "your kin" it stands with the Greek and against both MS B and the marginal note in MS B ("your neighbor/friend").

So there are cases in which the Masada Sirach manuscript agrees with the margin of MS B against MS B and the Greek, in which it agrees with MS B and the Greek against the margin of MS B, and in which it agrees with the Greek against MS B and its marginal note. Such agreements and disagreements are not sufficient to establish a stemma of manuscripts. Conjunctive errors are needed for that. But they do point to the fluid character of the text of Sirach at a very early stage in its transmission and suggest that one cannot rigidly follow one manuscript or version but rather must weigh carefully and critically all the textual evidence.

TEXT 2: GOD'S GLORY IN CREATION
(SIRACH 42:15–25 = MASADA v 1–16)

Text

42:15ab/v 1 Now I will recall the works of God, and what I have seen I will repeat. *42:15cd/2* By the word of the Lord – His works, and by an act of His favor – His teaching.

42:16/3 The sun shining over everything is revealed, and [the g]lory of the Lord fills His works. *42:17ab/4* The holy ones of the Lord are not able to recount His wonders. *42:17c/5* The Lord strengthens His hosts to stand firm before His glory. *42:18/6* The abyss and the heart He searches, and in their inmost place He understands. *42:18cd/7* For the Most High knows all [know]ledge, [and] He gazes on what is to be forever. *42:19/8* He discloses the changes [. . .] reveals the trace of hidden things. *42:20/9* Knowledge is not lacking from before Him, nor does any word pa[ss] away. *42:21ab/10* The might of [His] wisdom [. . .], one [. . .], *42:21cd/11* nothing added [. . .], no counselor. *42:22/12* Are not all His works delightful, even to a spark and a fleeting vision?

42:23/13 Everything lives and [. . .] forever, [. . . for] everything there is a need and everything is preserved. *42:24/14–15* All of them [. . .] corresponding to one another, and He did not make any of them [in vain]. *42:25/16* One with the other exchanges their good, [. . .]. Who can get enough of gazing on their splendor?

Exposition

Some of the best preserved parts of Sirach in the Masada Ben Sira scroll (cols v–vi) concern God's glory made manifest in creation. At this point in his book Ben Sira puts aside the role of the sage imparting practical advice and reflects on the glory of God made manifest in creation (42:15–43:33). The introductory poem (42:15–25) praises God's creation as "full of His glory" and reflects on God's omniscience and purpose in creation.

The idea of creation made "by the word of the Lord" (42:15c) echoes Genesis 1 and points forward to Sirach 43:26 ("by His word all things hold together"). The body of the poem (42:17–22) celebrates the omniscience and omnipotence of God. The final portion (42:23–25) contributes to Ben Sira's doctrine of modified dualism in creation (all things in pairs) found also in 33:7–15; 39:12–35; and 40:8–10.

This section of the Masada Sirach manuscript is noteworthy because in lines 7 and 12 it supplies the Hebrew texts for two couplets (42:18cd and 42:22) that are present in the Greek manuscript tradition but absent from the Hebrew MS B. That we now possess Hebrew versions for both these verses is a great gain. Yet in each case comparison with the Greek text suggests that the Greek translator may not have correctly understood the Hebrew text or perhaps used a slightly different Hebrew version.

In Sirach 42:18cd (= Masada MS v 7) Yadin read and translated the newly found Hebrew text as follows: "For the Most High possesseth (all) [knowledge, and] seeth what comes to eternity." In translating the Hebrew word ʾtywt as "what comes" Yadin correctly followed the lead of several passages in Isaiah (see 41:23; 44:7; 45:11). The Greek translation, however, presupposes a (mis)reading of ʾtywt ("what comes") as ʾwtwt ("signs"): " . . . and looks into the sign(s) of the age." The Greek version is awkward and hard to understand. The newly found Masada Hebrew text indicates that the Greek translator either misread ʾtywt as ʾwtwt or was working from a copy of Sirach in which the error ʾwtwt was already present.

In Sirach 42:22 (= Masada v 12) Yadin read the Hebrew so as to give the following translation: "All His works are lovely, (even) unto a spark and a fleeting vision." The first part presents no problem, but the second part does. In the translation of the second part Yadin was following the Greek version: ". . . and like a spark they are to see." But as John Strugnell (1969: 116–17) pointed out, this translation is not really parallel to the first part of the couplet, nor does it fit the context of the delightfulness and permanence of God's works set by Sirach 42:22–23. Instead, Strugnell proposed a different division of the Hebrew letters, which results in a perfectly parallel and sensible rendering of Sirach 42:22b: "delightful to gaze upon and a joy to behold." But of course if Strugnell is correct, then the Greek translator either had an incorrect Hebrew text with something like the reading proposed by Yadin or made the same kind of mistake that Yadin supposedly made.

TEXT 3: PRAISE OF "FAMOUS MEN"
(SIRACH 44:1–17 = MASADA vii 6–24)

Text

44:1/vii 6 [. . .] godly me[n], or father[s]. *44:2/7* Great glory
the Most High apportioned, and greatness [. . .].

44:3cd/8 [. . .] and counselors in their wise advice, and seers
of all in pro[phecy . . .], *44:4ab/9* rulers of the nation in their
planning, and princes in decree[s . . .], *44:4cd/10* the wise of
speech in their instruction, and speakers of proverbs [. . .],
44:5/11 composers of song according to rule, and authors of
[. . .], *44:6/12* men of valour and supported with strength
[. . .].

44:7/13 All these in their generation were glorified [. . .].
44:8/14 Some of them left behind a name [. . .], *44:9/15* and
some of them – there is no memory for him, [. . .], *44:9c* as
though they never were [. . .]. *44:10/17* But these were godly
men, and [. . .]. *44:11/18* If (= With) their offspring their
goodness remains firm, and [. . .], *44:12/19* in their covenant
their offspring stands, and their issue [. . .], *44:13/20* and unto
eternity their offspring will stand, and their glory will not be
blotted [out]; *44:14/21* their body in peace is buried, and their
name lives for generation and generation; *44:15/22* [. . .] a
congregation, and their praise an assembly recounts.

44:17/24 Noah the righteous was found perfect [. . .].

Exposition

The most famous part of the book of Sirach is the retelling of Israel's history in chapters 44–50 ("Now let us praise famous men").
The basic theme is that God's glory made manifest in creation (see
42:15–43:33) has also been made manifest in Israel's history from
the patriarchs to Simon the high priest about 200 BCE (Ben Sira's
own day).

The Masada Ben Sira manuscript breaks off with the introductory poem (44:1–15) and the mention of Noah (44:17). After intro-
ducing the theme of God as the one who portions out glory (44:1–
2), the poem lists various types of famous men (44:3–6) and reflects
on the immortality of the "good name" that lives on among God's
people (44:7–15). The catalogue of heroes then begins with Noah
(44:17).

In almost every verse only the first half is preserved. Nevertheless, what does remain illustrates another important feature of this manuscript: However good and valuable the Masada Sirach manuscript is, it also contains some errors and controversial readings.

From the list of types of famous men is missing the first two members: "Rulers of the earth in their kingdoms, and men of renown in their might" (44:3ab). The presence of this couplet is witnessed by the Hebrew manuscript B and the Greek tradition, and is guaranteed by the "and" before "counselors" in 42:3c (line 8). Also, in Sirach 44:11 (line 18) the obviously correct reading of the first word is "with" (*'m*), whereas the Masada manuscript has a meaningless "if" (*'m*) – a simple scribal error.

The omission of Sirach 44:16 with its mention of Enoch and the beginning of the catalogue of heroes with Noah present a more complicated textual problem. This may again be a case of a simple scribal error as with the two examples discussed above. Yet one of the longstanding textual puzzles of Sirach 44–50 is that Enoch gets two mentions (44:16 and 49:14). With its omission of the first reference to Enoch, the Masada manuscript may represent the better and more original version. Then the first Enoch reference (44:16) could be dismissed as a scribal addition made somewhere in the transmission process. Or the two references may have been intended by Ben Sira to form an inclusion at the beginning and end of his catalogue (before his description of Simon the high priest in chapter 50), and thus the Masada manuscript may be defective here also or perhaps even said to display an anti-Enoch tendency.

BIBLIOGRAPHICAL ESSAY

Throughout this book I have included references to editions of the Qumran wisdom texts and to scholarly studies on them. Full bibliographical data can be found in the bibliography that follows. Here I wish to call attention to certain books and articles that I regard as especially significant and that can serve as starting points for further study of the Qumran scrolls and the wisdom texts among them.

The general approach that I take to the Qumran scrolls is best expressed by F. M. Cross (my first teacher in the Qumran scrolls) in *The Ancient Library of Qumran*. Originally published in 1958, it remains a brilliant introduction. It has been slightly revised and expanded by a new chapter (Cross 1995). Solid and reliable information for a general audience is provided by J. A. Fitzmyer in *Responses to 101 Questions on the Dead Sea Scrolls* (Fitzmyer 1992b), and J. C. VanderKam in *The Dead Sea Scrolls Today* (1994). A fresh look at the Dead Sea scrolls from a Jewish perspective is given by L. H. Schiffman in *Reclaiming the Dead Sea Scrolls* (Schiffman 1994).

Good introductions to biblical wisdom literature are provided by J. L. Crenshaw in *Old Testament Wisdom* (Crenshaw 1981) and R. E. Murphy in *The Tree of Life* (Murphy 1990). Both authors have devoted much of their academic careers to the wisdom writings, and their syntheses for general audiences are excellent. The literary forms found in the biblical wisdom books are well analyzed by Murphy in *Wisdom Literature* (1981), part of a project entitled the "The Forms of the Old Testament Literature." Two collections of essays illustrate new directions in the study of wisdom literature: J. G. Gammie and L. Perdue (eds), *The Sage in Israel and the Ancient Near East* (1990), and Perdue *et al.* (eds), *In Search of Wisdom* (1993).

The Hebrew texts of the Qumran wisdom writings have appeared or will soon appear in the official publication series,

"Discoveries in the Judaean Desert" (DJD). Some biblical manuscripts of the wisdom books were published in early volumes, and the others are now in the process of publication. The Aramaic Targum of Job edited by J. P. M. van der Ploeg and A. S. van der Woude (1971) appeared outside the official series. The wisdom texts from the Cave 11 Psalms Scrolls were edited by J. A. Sanders (1965), and 4Q184 and 4Q185 were presented by J. M. Allegro (1968) – both in the DJD series. The Qumran wisdom texts treated in chapters 6 and 7 of this book will soon appear in the DJD series. In the meantime one can find preliminary Hebrew texts in the editions by B. Z. Wacholder and M. G. Abegg, *A Preliminary Edition of the Unpublished Dead Sea Scrolls*, vol. 2 (1991); and R. H. Eisenman and M. O. Wise, *The Dead Sea Scrolls Uncovered* (1992). The latter edition especially should be used with caution (Harrington and Strugnell 1993: 491–99). The Community Rule and the Thanksgiving Hymns (Hodayot) were among the first Qumran scrolls discovered and published, and their Hebrew texts can be found in many forms. Pointed Hebrew texts of 1QS (Community Rule) and 1QH (Hodayot) appear in *Die Texte aus Qumran* (Loshe 1964: 1–43, 109–75). A more recent edition of 1QS along with Cave 4 fragments of the Community Rule is presented in the first volume of *The Dead Sea Scrolls* (Charlesworth 1994: 1–108). Cave 4 fragments of Hodayot are the second volume of *A Preliminary Edition of the Unpublished Dead Sea Scolls* (Wacholder and Abegg 1991: 254–84). The Masada manuscript of Ben Sira was edited by Y. Yadin (1965).

English translations of many of the texts treated in this volume appear in F. García Martínez's *The Dead Sea Scrolls Translated* (1994) and G. Vermes' *The Dead Sea Scrolls in English* (4th rev. ed.; Vermes 1995). García Martínez gives more texts. Vermes' book is less expensive and more likely to be available at mass-market bookstores.

For a sober presentation of Jewish wisdom literature and of Jesus as a wisdom teacher and the wisdom of God, see B. C. Witherington's *Jesus the Sage* (1994). A good presentation of the wisdom stratum in Q in the context of ancient wisdom instructions is J. S. Kloppenborg's *The Formation of Q* (1987). The evidence for possible connections between Cynicism and early Christianity is gathered by F. G. Downing in *Cynics and Christian origins* (1992). The Q material and the Cynic connections are brought together by J. D. Crossan in *The Historical Jesus* (1991), B. L. Mack in *The Lost Gospel* (1993), and L. E. Vaage in *Galilean Upstarts* (1994). For a critique, see the article by Betz (1994: 453–75).

BIBLIOGRAPHY

ABBREVIATIONS

BASOR *Bulletin of the American Schools of Oriental Research*
BETL Bibliotheca Ephemeridum Theologicarum Lovaniensium
CBQ *Catholic Biblical Quarterly*
DJD Discoveries in the Judaean Desert
JBL *Journal of Biblical Literature*
JQR *Jewish Quarterly Review*
JSJ *Journal for the Study of Judaism*
JSS *Journal of Semitic Studies*
RB *Revue Biblique*
RQ *Revue de Qumrân*
SNTSMS Society for New Testament Studies Monograph Series
ZAW *Zeitschrift für die alttestamentliche Wissenschaft*

WORKS

Allegro, J. M. (1964) "The Wiles of the Wicked Woman, a Sapiential Work from Qumran's Fourth Cave," *Palestine Exploration Quarterly* 96: 53–55.

—— (1968) *Qumrân Cave 4. I (4Q158–4Q186)* (DJD 5), Oxford: Clarendon Press.

Baillet, M., Milik, J. T., and de Vaux, R. (1962) *Les "petites grottes" de Qumrân* (DJD 3), Oxford: Clarendon Press.

Baumgarten J. M. (1991) "On the Nature of the Seductress in 4Q184," *RQ* 15: 133–43.

Betz, H. D. (1994) "Jesus and the Cynics: Survey and Analysis of a Hypothesis," *Journal of Religion* 74: 453–75.

Brooke, G. J. (1989) "The Wisdom of Matthew's Beatitudes (4QBeat and Mt. 5:3–12)," *Scripture Bulletin* 19: 35–41.

Broshi, M. (1983) "Beware the Wiles of the Wanton Woman," *Biblical Archaeology Review* 9/4: 54–56.

Brown, R. E. (1968) *The Semitic Background of the Term "Mystery" in the New Testament*, Philadelphia: Fortress.

Burgmann, H. (1974) "'The Wicked Woman': Der Makkabäer Simon?" *RQ* 8: 323–59.

Byrskog, S. (1994) *Jesus the Only Teacher. Didactic Authority and Transmission in Ancient Israel, Ancient Judaism and the Matthean Community*, Stockholm: Almqvist & Wiksell.

Charlesworth, J. H. (ed.) (1994) *The Dead Sea Scrolls. Hebrew, Aramaic, and Greek Texts with English Translations*, vol. 1, Tübingen: Mohr-Siebeck; Louisville: Westminster John Knox.

Chyutin, M. (1994) "The Redaction of the Qumranic and the Traditional Book of Psalms as a Calendar," *RQ* 16: 367–95.

Clements, R. E. (1992) *Wisdom in Theology*, Carlisle, UK: Paternoster; Grand Rapids: Eerdmans.

Coppens, J. (1990) "'Mystery' in the Theology of Saint Paul and its Parallels at Qumran," in J. Murphy-O'Connor and J. H. Charlesworth (eds), *Paul and the Dead Sea Scrolls*, New York: Crossroad, pp. 132–58.

Crenshaw, J. L. (1981) *Old Testament Wisdom. An Introduction*, Atlanta: John Knox.

Cross, F. M. (1995) *The Ancient Library of Qumran*, rev. ed., Minneapolis: Fortress.

Crossan, J. D. (1991) *The Historical Jesus. The Life of a Mediterranean Jewish Peasant*, San Francisco: HarperCollins.

Denis, A.-M. (1967) *Les thèmes de connaissance dans le Document de Damas*, Studia Hellenistica 15, Louvain: Publications Universitaires.

Deutsch, C. (1982) "The Sirach 51 Acrostic: Confession and Exhortation," *ZAW* 94: 400–9.

—— (1987) *Hidden Wisdom and the Easy Yoke. Torah and Discipleship in Matthew 11.25–30*, Sheffield: JSOT Press.

Downing, F. G. (1992) *Cynics and Christian Origins*, Edinburgh: T. & T. Clark.

Duhaime, J. L. (1987) "Dualistic Reworking in the Scrolls from Qumran," *CBQ* 49: 32–56.

—— (1988) "Le dualisme de Qumrân et la littérature de sagesse vétérotestamentaire," *Église et Théologie* 19: 401–22.

Eisenman, R. H. and Wise, M. O. (1992) *The Dead Sea Scrolls Uncovered. The First Complete Translation and Interpretation of 50 Key Documents Withheld for Over 35 Years*, Shaftesbury, UK, Rockport, MA, and Brisbane: Element.

Elgvin, T. (1993) "Admonition Texts from Qumran Cave 4," in M. O. Wise *et al.* (eds), *Methods of Investigation of the Dead Sea Scrolls and the Khirbet Qumran Site. Present Realities and Future Prospects*, New York: Academy of Arts and Sciences, pp. 137–52.

—— (1995a) "Wisdom, Revelation, and Eschatology in an Early Essene Writing," in E. H. Lovering (ed), *Society of Biblical Literature 1995 Seminar Papers*, Atlanta: Scholars Press, pp. 440–63.

—— (1995b) "The Reconstruction of Sapiential Work A," *RQ* 16: 559–80.

Fitzmyer, J. A. (1974) "Some Observations on the Targum of Job from Qumran Cave 11," *CBQ* 36: 503–24; see also (1977) *A Wandering Aramean. Collected Aramaic Essays*, Missoula: Scholars Press, pp. 161–82.

—— (1992a) "A Palestinian Collection of Beatitudes," in F. van Segbroeck *et al.* (eds), *The Four Gospels 1992. Festschrift Frans Neirynck*, Leuven: Leuven University Press and Peeters, pp. 509–15.

—— (1992b) *Responses to 101 Questions on the Dead Sea Scrolls*, New York and Mahwah, NJ: Paulist.

Gammie, J. G. and Perdue, L. (eds) (1990) *The Sage in Israel and the Ancient Near East*, Winona Lake, IN: Eisenbrauns.

García Martínez, F. (1994) *The Dead Sea Scrolls Translated. The Qumran Texts in English*, trans. W. G. W. Watson, Leiden: Brill.

Gazov-Ginzberg, A. M. (1967) "Double Meaning in a Qumran Work ('The Wiles of the Wicked Woman')," *RQ* 6: 279–85.

Harrington, D. J. (1994) "Wisdom at Qumran," in E. Ulrich and J. VanderKam (eds), *The Community of the Renewed Covenant. The Notre Dame Symposium on the Dead Sea Scrolls*, Notre Dame, IN: University of Notre Dame Press, pp. 137–52.

—— (1996) "The *Rāz Nihyeh* in a Qumran Wisdom Text (1Q26, 4Q415–418, 423)," *RQ* 17.

—— and Strugnell, J. (1993) "Qumran Cave 4 Texts: A New Publication," *JBL* 112: 491–99.

Hengel, M. (1974) *Judaism and Hellenism*, vol. 1, Philadelphia: Fortress, pp. 218–24.

Holm-Nielsen, S. (1960) *Hodayot. Psalms from Qumran*, Aarhus: Universitetsforlaget.

Jongeling, B. (1972) "Contributions of the Qumran Job Targum to the Aramaic Vocabulary," *JSS* 17: 191–97.

Kister, M. (1994) "Commentary to 4Q298," *JQR* 85: 237–49.

Kittel, B. (1981) *The Hymns of Qumran: Translation and Commentary*, Chico, CA: Scholars.

Kloppenborg, J. S. (1987) *The Formation of Q: Trajectories in Ancient Wisdom Collections*, Philadelphia: Fortress.

Knibb, M. (1984) "1 Enoch," in H. F. D. Sparks (ed.), *The Apocryphal Old Testament*, Oxford: Clarendon Press, pp. 169–319.

Kosmala, H. (1973) "Maskil," *Journal of the Ancient Near East Society* 5: 235–41.

Lange, A. (1995a) *Weisheit und Prädestination*, Leiden: Brill.

—— (1995b) "Wisdom and Predestination in the Dead Sea Scrolls," *Dead Sea Discoveries* 2: 340–54.

Leaney, A. R. C. (1966) *The Rule of the Community*, London: SCM.

Lehmann, M. R. (1961) "Ben Sira and the Qumran Literature," *RQ* 3: 103–16.

—— (1983) "11 Q Psᵃ and Ben Sira," *RQ* 11:239–51.

Lichtenberger, H. (1978) "Eine weisheitliche Mahnrede in den Qumranfunde (4Q185)," in M. Delcor (ed.), *Qumrân. Sa piété, sa théologie et son milieu* (BETL 46), Paris and Gembloux: Duculot; Leuven: Leuven University Press, pp. 151–62.

Lipscomb, W. L. and Sanders, J. A. (1977) "Wisdom at Qumran," in J. G. Gammie *et al.* (eds), *Israelite Wisdom. Theological and Literary Essays in Honor of Samuel Terrien*, Missoula: Scholars Press, pp. 277–85.

Lohse, E. (1964) *Die Texte aus Qumran. Hebräisch und deutsch*, Munich: Kösel.

Mack, B. L. (1993) *The Lost Gospel: The Book of Q and Christian Origins*, San Francisco: HarperCollins.

Milik, J. T. (1976) *The Books of Enoch, Aramaic Fragments of Qumrân Cave 4*, Oxford: Clarendon Press.

—— (1977) *Qumrân Grotte 4. II* (DJD 6), Oxford: Clarendon Press.

—— (1992) "Les modèles araméens du livre d'Esther dans la Grotte 4 de Qumrân," *RQ* 15: 321–99.

—— and Barthélemy, D. (1955) *Qumran Cave I* (DJD 1), Oxford: Clarendon Press.

Moore, R. D. (1981) "Personification of the Seduction of Evil: 'The Wiles of the Wicked Woman,'" *RQ* 10: 505–19.

Muilenberg, J. (1954) "A Qoheleth Scroll from Qumran," *BASOR* 135: 20–28.

Muraoka, T. (1979) "Sir. 51: 13–30: An Erotic Hymn to Wisdom?" *JSJ* 10: 166–78.

Murphy, R. E. (1981) *Wisdom Literature*, The Forms of the Old Testament Literature 13, Grand Rapids: Eerdmans.

—— (1990) *The Tree of Life. An Exploration of Biblical Wisdom Literature*, New York: Doubleday.

Nebe, G. W. (1994) "Qumranica I: Zu unveröffentlichten Handschriften aus Höhle von Qumran," *ZAW* 106: 307–22.

Newsom, C. A. (1990a) "The Sage in the Literature of Qumran: The Functions of the *Maskil*," in J. G. Gammie and L. Perdue (eds), *The Sage in Israel and the Ancient Near East*, Winona Lake, IN: Eisenbrauns, pp. 373–82.

—— (1990b) "'Sectually Explicit' Literature from Qumran," in W. Propp *et al.* (eds), *The Hebrew Bible and Its Interpreters*, Winona Lake, IN: Eisenbrauns, pp. 167–87.

Perdue, L. (1986) "The Wisdom Sayings of Jesus," *Forum* 2/3: 3–35.

—— *et al.* (eds) (1993) *In Search of Wisdom*, Louisville: Westminster/Knox.

Pfann, S. (1994) "4Q298: The Maskil's Address to All Sons of Dawn," *JQR* 85: 203–35.

Piper, R. A. (1989) *Wisdom in the Q-Tradition. The Aphoristic Teaching of Jesus* (SNTSMS 61), Cambridge: Cambridge University Press.

Puech, E. (1991) "4Q525 et les péricopes des béatitudes en Ben Sira et Matthieu," *RB* 98: 80–106.

Rigaux, B. (1957–58) "Révélation des mystères et perfection à Qumrân et dans le Nouveau Testament," *New Testament Studies* 4: 237–62.

Ringgren, H. (1995) *The Faith of Qumran. Theology of the Dead Sea Scrolls (Expanded Edition)*, New York: Crossroad.

Sanders, J. A. (1965) *The Psalms Scrolls of Qumrân Cave 11 (11QPsa)* (DJD 4), Oxford: Clarendon Press.

—— (1967) *The Dead Sea Psalms Scroll*, Ithaca, NY: Cornell University Press.

Schiffman, L. H. (1993) "'4Q Mysteries^b,' A Preliminary Edition," *RQ* 16: 203–23.

—— (1994) *Reclaiming the Dead Sea Scrolls. The History of Judaism, the*

Background of Christianity, the Lost Library of Qumran, Philadelphia and Jerusalem: Jewish Publication Society.

—— (1995) "4Q Mysteries^a: A Preliminary Edition and Translation," in Z. Zevit *et al.* (eds), *Solving Riddles and Untying Knots: Biblical, Epigraphic, and Semitic Studies in Honor of Jonas C. Greenfield*, Winona Lake, IN: Eisenbrauns, pp. 207–60.

Scott, M. (1992) *Sophia and the Johannine Jesus*, Sheffield: JSOT Press.

Skehan, P. W. and Di Lella, A. A. (1987) *The Wisdom of Ben Sira* (Anchor Bible), New York: Doubleday.

Skehan P. W., Ulrich, E., and Sanderson, J. E. (1992) *Qumrân Cave 4. IV: Palaeo-Hebrew and Greek Biblical Manuscripts* (DJD 9), Oxford: Clarendon Press.

Sokoloff, M. (1974) *The Targum to Job from Qumran Cave XI*, Ramat Gan: Bar-Ilan University Press.

Strugnell, J. (1969) "Notes and Queries on 'The Ben Sira Scroll from Masada,'" in A. Malamat (ed.), *Eretz Israel IX: W. F. Albright Volume*, Jerusalem: Israel Exploration Society, pp. 109–19.

—— (1970) "Notes en marge du volume V des 'Discoveries in the Judaean Desert of Jordan,'" *RQ* 7: 163–276.

Suggs, M. J. (1970) *Wisdom, Christology, and Law in Matthew's Gospel*, Cambridge, MA: Harvard University Press.

Talmon, S. (1994) "The Community of the Renewed Covenant: Between Judaism and Christianity," in E. Ulrich and J. VanderKam (eds), *The Community of the Renewed Covenant: The Notre Dame Symposium on the Dead Sea Scrolls*, Notre Dame, IN: Notre Dame University Press, pp. 3–24.

Tanzer, S. J. (1987) "The Sages at Qumran: Wisdom in the *Hodayot*," Ph.D. Dissertation, Harvard University.

Tobin, T. H. (1990) "4Q185 and Jewish Wisdom Literature," in H. W. Attridge *et al.* (eds), *Of Scribes and Scrolls* (Festschrift for J. Strugnell), Lanham, MD, New York, and London: University Press of America, pp. 145–52.

Tov, E. (1992) *Textual Criticism of the Hebrew Bible*, Minneapolis: Fortress.

Ulrich, E. (1995) "An Index of the Passages in the Biblical Manuscripts from the Judean Desert (Part 2: Isaiah–Chronicles)," *Dead Sea Discoveries* 2: 86–107.

Vaage, L. E. (1994) *Galilean Upstarts: Jesus' First Followers according to Q*, Valley Forge, PA: Trinity Press International.

VanderKam, J. C. (1994) *The Dead Sea Scrolls Today*, Grand Rapids: Eerdmans.

van der Ploeg, J. P. M. and van der Woude, A. S. (1971) *Le Targum de Job de la Grotte XI de Qumrân*, Leiden: Brill.

Vermes, G. (1995) *The Dead Sea Scrolls in English* (4th rev. ed.), Harmondsworth: Penguin.

Viviano, B. T. (1992) "Beatitudes Found Among the Dead Sea Scrolls," *Biblical Archaeology Review* 18/6: 53–55, 66.

—— (1993) "Eight Beatitudes at Qumran and in Matthew? A New Publication from Cave Four," *Svensk Exegetisk Årsbok* 58: 71–84.

Wacholder, B. Z. and Abegg, M. G. (1991) *A Preliminary Edition of the*

Unpublished Dead Sea Scrolls: The Hebrew and Aramaic Texts from Cave Four. Fascicle Two, Washington, DC: Biblical Archaeology Society.

Weiss, R. (1974) "Further Notes on the Qumran Targum to Job," *JSS* 19: 13–18.

Westermann, C. (1994) *Roots of Wisdom. The Oldest Proverbs of Israel and Other Peoples*, Louisville: Westminster/John Knox.

Willett, M. E. (1992) *Wisdom Christology in the Fourth Gospel*, San Francisco: Mellen.

Winton, A. P. (1990) *The Proverbs of Jesus. Issues of History and Rhetoric*, Sheffield, JSOT.

Witherington, B. C. (1994) *Jesus the Sage. The Pilgrimage of Wisdom*, Minneapolis: Fortress.

Worrell, J. E. (1968) "Concepts of Wisdom in the Dead Sea Scrolls," Ph.D. Dissertation, Claremont Graduate School.

Yadin, Y. (1965) *The Ben Sira Scroll from Masada*, Jerusalem: Israel Exploration Society.

INDEX OF SUBJECTS

INDEX OF REFERENCES TO BIBLICAL AND OTHER ANCIENT LITERATURE

RABBINIC LITERATURE

DATE DUE
